REDISCOVERY OF THE ORDINARY

FOR MPHO AND THE CHILDREN

REDISCOVERY OF THE ORDINARY
❖ ❖ ❖

ESSAYS ON SOUTH AFRICAN
LITERATURE
AND
CULTURE

NJABULO S. NDEBELE

UNIVERSITY OF KWAZULU-NATAL PRESS

Published in 2006 by University of KwaZulu-Natal Press
Private Bag X01, Scottsville, 3209
South Africa
Email: books@ukzn.ac.za
Website: www.ukznpress.co.za

Originally published by COSAW, 1991

ISBN 1-86914-079-6

Editor: Andrea Nattrass
Typesetter: Patricia Comrie
Cover: Sebastien Quevauvilliers, Flying Ant Designs
Cover photograph of Njabulo S. Ndebele courtesy of the University of Cape Town

Printed and bound by Interpak Books, Pietermaritzburg

CONTENTS

Foreword by Michael Chapman vii

1. Turkish Tales and Some Thoughts
   on South African Fiction 1

2. The Rediscovery of the Ordinary:
   Some New Writings in South Africa 31

3. Redefining Relevance 55

4. Actors and Interpreters:
   Popular Culture and Progressive Formalism 73

5. The English Language and
   Social Change in South Africa 101

6. Towards Progressive Cultural Planning 125

7. Against Pamphleteering the Future 141

8. The Writers' Movement in South Africa 155

   APPENDICES

9. The Noma Award Acceptance Speech 169

10. Interview with Njabulo S. Ndebele 173

FOREWORD

Njabulo S. Ndebele's essays on South African literature and culture appeared initially in various South African and overseas journals and magazines in the 1980s. They encompass a period of trauma, defiance, and change: the decade of the collapse of apartheid and the challenge of reconstructing a future. In 1991, the essays were collected under the current title of *Rediscovery of the Ordinary: Essays on South African Literature and Culture*.[1] In this book these essays are reprinted without revision, together with an interview[2] provoked by Albie Sachs's paper 'Preparing Ourselves for Freedom'.[3]

That it is possible to republish the essays without revision fifteen years after their first appearance in accessible collected form is a tribute to Ndebele's prescience. The issues that he raises and the questions that he poses remain key to a people who, after apartheid, are seeking to rediscover the complex ordinariness of living in a civil society. Of the character of literary culture in such a pursuit Ndebele is uncompromising: literature offers 'inventiveness of treatment', 'sharpening of insight', and 'deepening of consciousness'.[4] Whether in Solomon T. Plaatje's political commentary, the *Drum* stories of the 1950s, or – he was too modest to invoke his own creative achievement – in his fiction, *Fools and Other Stories* (1983) or, more recently, *The Cry of Winnie Mandela* (2003),[5] Ndebele eschews the surface representations of oppression. Instead of stereotype or agitprop, he presents the imaginative and ethical potential of our human conduct.

To return to the essays so many years later is to realise that Ndebele's perceptions were not always fully grasped even by those who supported his critique of the politics of spectacle: his critique of the 'over-determined' South African social and cultural scene of the 1980s. The error was to interpret his concern with the spectacular as an implicit endorsement of its apparent opposite: the psychological mind-set of Western-style individualism. Ndebele's understandings, in consequence, were placed by several critics in dichotomous relationships: art versus politics; and the personal versus the public. But these were not Ndebele's dichotomies. His strenuous formulations still await the full justice of their possibilities. As he himself phrases his qualification of categories in the essay 'Actors and Interpreters': 'our writers must constantly assess their level of understanding of society'; they must 'cultivate a total interest in their community'; and 'their definition of what constitutes politics must be as inclusive as possible', for 'real fiction . . . is creative discussion of real social issues'. Or, as he refuses to entertain division between the 'elite' work and the 'popular' expression: 'The written word, being so central to the experience of the modern world, and the vast possibilities for intellectual development that it offers, must be brought to the centre of modern popular consciousness.'[6]

Here imaginative and ethical responsibilities are inseparable; the writer is simultaneously an artist and an educator. As South Africa defines and redefines its legacies, Njabulo S. Ndebele's critical intelligence continues to sound its contemporary relevance.

Michael Chapman
University of KwaZulu-Natal, January 2006

NOTES

1. Njabulo S. Ndebele, *Rediscovery of the Ordinary: Essays on South African Literature and Culture* (Johannesburg: COSAW, 1991).

2. 'Njabulo Ndebele'. In *Exchanges: South African Writing in Transition*, edited by Duncan Brown and Bruno van Dyk (Pietermaritzburg: University of Natal Press, 1991, pp.49–57).

3. Albie Sachs, 'Preparing Ourselves for Freedom'. In *Spring is Rebellious: Arguments about Cultural Freedom by Albie Sachs and Respondents*, edited by Ingrid de Kock and Karen Press (Cape Town: Buchu Books, 1990, pp.19–29).

4. 'The Noma Award Acceptance Speech' (p.172 of this book).

5. Njabulo S. Ndebele, *Fools and Other Stories* (Johannesburg: Ravan Press, 1983); *The Cry of Winnie Mandela* (Cape Town: David Philip, 2003).

6. 'Actors and Interpreters: Popular Culture and Progressive Formalism' (p.97 of this book).

1

❖ ❖ ❖

TURKISH TALES AND SOME THOUGHTS ON SOUTH AFRICAN FICTION

As I was preparing this review of Yashar Kemal's *Anatolian Tales*,[1] I realised that I was going to have to go beyond the conventional length and treatment. The subject matter of Kemal's stories and the forcefulness of his storytelling, left me thinking long and hard about his art. It dawned on me that I had before me a collection of compelling artistic statements which at the same time presented themselves, with an intriguing sense of inevitability, as fruitful occasions for a serious examination of key social issues affecting some rural and semi-rural communities in one 'Third World' country, Turkey. There seemed to be something disturbingly familiar about these stories; something the echoes of which edged the focus of my mind towards the South African literary situation, where it seemed there was something missing. Was there, in contemporary South African fiction, a tradition of such compelling and imaginative recreation of rural life as in Kemal's stories? I could not come up with ready examples. On the contrary, instead of showing any serious interest in rural life, our writers seemed decidedly preoccupied with urban culture. Granted that such preoccupation may be justified and valid, what, nevertheless, was the state of the resulting urban fiction itself as art? Before I address myself to the questions posed, let me describe what triggered them off in the first place.

1

I

Kemal's *Anatolian Tales* is a collection of stories in which we are treated to a detailed, imaginative recreation of rural life in the Anatolian plains of Turkey. It consists of four fairly long, and three very short stories. I will summarise the long stories first.

'A Dirty Story', which opens the collection, is the story of Hollow Osman, a somewhat mentally retarded peasant who has been living with and working for Huru, a woman who has brought him up since he was a child. Osman's friends succeed in convincing him to persuade Huru to buy him a wife. After all, hasn't Osman been 'slaving' for Huru all these years, and 'living alone and sleeping in barns like a dog'? But it is not long after Osman has had a wife purchased for him that a rich landowner's son seduces her. Soon, the young men of the village are 'lining up at her door all through the night'.

Osman is powerless to deal with the humiliation. Things come to a head when even vital economic activity, such as ploughing, stops, threatening the village with virtual starvation. The young men return from Osman's house in the morning to sleep, too tired to do any work. The village faces a crisis. In a plot involving the Agha (landlord) and some other people, Osman's wife is driven out of the village. But the young men pursue her to her place of refuge, where they continue to ravish her mercilessly. In the end, Osman picks her up, all but lifeless, and runs away with her.

'Drumming Out' is about Fikret Irmakli Bey, a young man recently graduated from the university whose first appointment is as District Commissioner in Anatolia. Learning of his appointment, all the rich farmers of the district prepare to give the new Commissioner a glorious welcome, and they provide him with the best accommodation available. The aim is to lull the young, in-experienced Commissioner into a stupor of comfort and complacency, so that he could easily issue permits for rice planting against the Rice Commission's regulations which are meant to protect public health. Bey falls into the trap, and planting permits are issued liberally. Matters come to a head when powerless villagers are flooded out of their houses. As a result, a conscience-stricken Deputy Commissioner, who has been working in the district for a long time, brings the attention of the new Commissioner to the regulations. The Commissioner, to his horror, realises too late that he has been fooled. From that moment, he begins his fight against the Aghas, and goes out of his way to protect and defend the interests of the peasants. The rest of the story is about the determined efforts of the Aghas to get rid of the Commissioner, who is no longer their 'friend'. They succeed. The final ejection ceremony is the 'drumming-out' by an 'army of small boys, each one holding a tin can and drumming on it with all his might'. 'It's a send off', it is explained to the departing Commissioner. 'The Aghas always do that for Government officials forced to go like you . . .' Thus, the Commissioner leaves, but he has won the gratitude of the peasants.

In 'The Baby', Kemal tells the story of Ismail, whose wife has just died, leaving her husband with a newly born baby. Ismail's problem is how to bring the child up in so desolate a place as his village. He also has to deal with unfounded recriminations that he contributed directly to the death of his wife. Ismail goes around trying to get the help of breast-feeding women. But only one person is willing to help: a blind woman who 'sees' more clearly than others. But her help is of no avail. There is no relief from the hunger and suffering. The rest of the story is a piling up of details of Ismail's suffering.

In 'The Shopkeeper', the last of the long stories, Mehmet is a village storekeeper whose store is also some kind of village social centre. Men gather there for a chat. But always there with them is Queer Sully, a boy who always sits, absolutely silent, a few paces away from the men. Part of Mehmet's business is to obtain grain clandestinely from village women who, without the knowledge of their husbands, want to buy a few luxury items from the store. This way, Mehmet accumulates a lot of grain which will seemingly bring in a lot of money when household stocks run out. An unscrupulous businessman, Mehmet deals underhandedly with his competitors. He also arranges abductions of village girls for men in the cities. But Mehmet has to reckon with Queer Sully who has a quiet disdain for injustice. He has a history of dealing firmly with local wrong-doers setting their fields on fire, for example. Mehmet tries to ward off possible retribution by attempting to bribe Queer Sully with the bounty of the store. At the end of the story, Sully almost clears the store of goods, and then spits in the shopkeeper's face, for Mehmet had just arranged for the beating up of a competitor.

The next three stories are the short ones. 'White Trousers' is the story of a young apprentice who dreams of owning a pair of white trousers. He lives with his widowed mother and already shoulders the heavy responsibility of helping her in the hard task of surviving. The boy's resolve to prove himself as a worthy and deserving worker is severely tested when he is hired out to work continuously for three days at a kiln. He barely passes the test, and a fine relationship develops between him and his employer. In the manner of a rites of passage story, the boy is well on the way to being an economic asset to himself and his mother.

'On the Road' is the story of a man who returns home from the market where he has just sold six sacks of farm produce. He is riding home on his donkey cart, and is counting his money, when he comes across a woman walking alone in the scorching sun, along the empty country road. He offers her a ride. It turns out that she is returning home after a divorce. Two lonely people meet on a lonely road. Fate brings them together for a lifelong companionship.

In 'Green Onions', Mahmud is returning home to his village after being away to make money in the cities for five years, so that he could set himself up in livestock farming. His return home by train is also his second train ride. In the compartment, he finds a young man with a sleeping, sickly woman resting her head on the young man's shoulder. She has a 'wasting disease which, according to one doctor, can be cured by the breathing of fresh air full of the smell of pine trees'. The smell of fresh onions in the compartment so reminds Mahmud of his own village that he buys fresh green onions at the next station. The green onions become a symbol of all that is wonderful in the world. Once he learns of the young woman's problem, Mahmud wants to share with the engaged couple the healing powers of the pines of his village, and its health-giving springs. There, they will find life, the girl will be cured and they will be married. Mahmud invites the couple to come and live with him. He will take care of them with the money he has just made and shower them with the hospitality of his village.

As the story ends the train is moving. The couple have got off at their village station and Mahmud is yelling the name of his village at them from the window of the departing train. In his excitement he had forgotten to give the name of his village to them.

II

A remarkable feature of Kemal's work in this collection, something I found refreshing, is that he emerges as a writer who is rooted firmly in the timeless tradition of storytelling. A chief characteristic of this tradition is that a story is allowed to unfold by itself with a minimum of authorial intervention through which a storyteller might directly suggest how readers or listeners should understand his story. Two key effects result from the lack of such intervention. Firstly, the entertainment value of the story is enhanced, and the emotional involvement of the reader is thus assured. Secondly, such involvement does not necessarily lead to a lulling of the reader's critical consciousness, as Brecht, the German poet and dramatist, would assert. On the contrary, the reader's emotional involvement in a well-told story triggers off an imaginative participation in which the reader recreates the story in his own mind, and is thus led to draw conclusions about the meaning of the story from the engaging logic of events as they are *acted out* in the story.

Also, there is an impersonal ring to Kemal's stories, one which approximates the impersonal, communal quality of a traditional tale of unknown origins passed from mouth to mouth.[2] This quality in Kemal's stories surely blends well with the Anatolian setting in which the oral tradition must still be alive. In both 'A Dirty Story' and

'The Shopkeeper' people often come together to exchange stories, even if some of the stories are gossip. For Kemal then, an observation by Walter Benjamin is most appropriate. Benjamin comments that 'experience which is passed from mouth to mouth is the source from which all storytellers have drawn. And among those who have written down the tales, it is the great ones whose written version differs least from the speech of the many nameless storytellers'.[3] Kemal, of course, does not appear in these stories to have written down known tales in the same way as A.C. Jordan did in his *Tales from Southern Africa*. But there is some evidence that Kemal is writing within a popular tradition he is doubtlessly conscious of. Andrew Mango observes that:

> Turkish 'socialist realist' theatrical writing of today, with its stock types of wicked landowners, downtrodden peasants and progressive intellectuals, derives . . . from a local tradition of popular pantomimes (called tuluat theatre) . . . Turkey's most successful novel of recent years, Yashar Kemal's *Ince Mehmet* (translated as *Mehmet, My Hawk*) is, for all its progressive message, a *destan*, a tale of stirring deeds by a local hero, *as told by generations of bazaar storytellers*. [My emphasis].[4]

Kemal's art then, is rooted in the history of storytelling in Anatolia. Perhaps his remarkable achievement can, to a very large extent, be attributed to this fact. I would now like to highlight some features of Kemal's art in *Anatolian Tales*.

A distinctive feature of Kemal's art is the apparent ease with which he opens his stories. The opening to 'A Dirty Story' for example, is instructive in this regard:

> The three of them were sitting on the damp earth, their backs against the dung-daubed brush-wall and their knees drawn up to their chests, when another man walked up and crouched beside them.

'Have you heard?' said one of them excitedly. 'Broken-Nose Jabbar's done it again! You know Jabbar, the fellow who brings all those women from the mountain villages and sells them in the plain? Well, this time he's come down with a couple of real beauties. The lads of Misdik have got together and bought one of them on the spot, and now they're having fun making her dance and all that . . . It's unbelievable! Where does the fellow find so many women? How does he get them to come with him? He's the devil's own son, he is . . .'

'Well, that's how he makes a living,' commented one of the men. 'Ever since I can remember, this Jabbar's been peddling women for the villages of the Chukurova plain. Allah provides for all and sundry . . .'

The ease of exposition coincides with the ironic ease with which a dehumanising abnormality, the turning of women into mere objects of commerce, has become normal. This creates an ambiguity within the reader, the kind of tense ambiguity which makes for reading enjoyment, in which the narrative style appears to validate an objective social condition which, at the same time, begs to be condemned. Kemal, therefore, dooms us to 'enjoy' injustice as we condemn it. This is a critical tension that stays with us throughout the story. In other words, we accept, as readers, the human validity of the situation before us while asking, at the same time, what terrible social conditions can produce such human beings. The irresistible sense of story, together with the detailed social realism, immediately engage us on two levels: that of imaginative involvement and enjoyment on the one hand, and critical evaluation on the other.

I would like to cite one more passage from 'A Dirty Story' which will help us understand other aspects of Kemal's narrative style. The following passage illustrates how he develops setting, character, dialogue and suggestive symbols for narrative effects:

Down in the villages of the Chukurova plain a sure sign of oncoming spring is when the women are seen with their heads on one another's lap, picking the lice out of one another's hair. So it was, on one of the first warm days of the year. A balmy sun shone carelessly down on the fields and women were sitting before their huts on the dusty ground, busy with the lice and wagging their tongues for all they were worth. An acrid odour of sweat hung about the group. Seedy Doneh was rummaging in the hair of a large woman who was stretched full length on the ground. She decided that she had been silent long enough.

'No,' she declared, 'it's not as you say, sister! He didn't force her or anything. She simply saw those shiny yellow boots. If you're going to believe Huru! . . . She's got to deny it, of course . . .'

The women are gossiping about the Agha's seduction of Hollow Osman's wife. Their dialogue complements their action: the gossip is as pleasurable as the 'picking of lice out of one another's hair'. In this way, the sense of community among the women is sealed, for better or for worse. This sisterhood breaks up sometimes, as when they fail to realise that the practice of wife buying undermines their own dignity. What is normal to the men, as we have seen, is normal to the women too. For example, the women's inability to sympathise with Osman's wife during her terrible ordeal makes them cruel witnesses. The sisterhood breaks up again when in 'The Baby' the women fail to come to the aid of one of them who dies in childbirth, leaving the baby in the care of a helpless man who wanders all over the desolate plains in search of someone kind enough to breast-feed his child. But sometimes, as in 'Drumming-Out', the sisterhood can rise to heroic proportions in the fight against the injustice threatening their very lives.

Another feature of the passage quoted above is how it depicts the human tendency to adjust social habits according to changing seasons. Indeed, in all of Kemal's stories we are made conscious of seasons, particularly summer. The hot sun becomes the summer's predominant image. So are the hot dry land and the dust. These

conditions are an ever present background to the people's consciousness. Nevertheless, they go about their business, and as
everywhere, are attempting to bring some semblance of meaning into
their lives.

There is also the omnipresent wealth and power of the
landowners, the Aghas, whose corruption is probably the most
predominant political-economic concern in the plains of Anatolia.
In a society that hovers precariously between feudalism and
capitalism, the owner of land, the ultimate source of the means of
survival, wields almost unlimited power. He can ruin land for profit
('Drumming-Out'); he can kill off competition ('Drumming-Out' and
'The Shopkeeper'); he can bribe government either with money or
with high sounding patriotic phrases, and he can seduce women
with impunity. Kemal, almost unobtrusively, dots here and there
the symbols of the Aghas' wealth: shiny yellow boots, white trousers,
and brand new cars. It is germane to point out that a lesser writer
would probably have been tempted, in order to 'strike a blow' for
justice, to dwell overly on these symbols, thus getting out of us
more indignation, and less understanding. Kemal is more interested
in the actual social processes of injustice than in finished products.
He *dramatises* these processes with much skill, allowing the nefarious
activities of the Aghas to *condemn themselves*.

Overall, *Anatolian Tales* is an unsentimental yet sympathetic
portrayal of peasant life with all its jealousies, vindictiveness and
cruelty, its powerlessness in the face of the wealthy, and in the ease
with which peasant solidarity can break up under stress. But all
those foibles are brought out under the control of the writer's deep
creative understanding of his subjects. The peasants are never seen
as debased human ghosts inviting only condescending sympathy or
pity. They are too disturbingly human for that. The realistic setting,
moreover, enables us to understand that the peasant condition is
not attributable to some mysterious forces constituting the 'human
condition'. They are what they are largely as a result of a particular
kind of life in a given set of physical conditions. Some triumph
against these conditions; others are destroyed by them. The result

of all this, for the reader, is a kind of understanding that is much deeper than any direct 'message' or 'instruction'. Deeper, because the stories are an occasion not for easy messages, but for asking further questions.

The endings of all Kemal's stories in this collection, leave us thinking. In the lengthy stories, the ending comes with defeat, and we leave the stories with an uncomfortable feeling of gloom. But this gloom is always accompanied by a kind of quiet, contemplative indignation. There is no resignation, only a quiet determination to find answers. The shorter stories on the other hand, share a rare kind of lyrical triumph. But the lyricism is never allowed to become sentimental. It is always grounded in the actual needs of survival; the cart and the reeds in 'On the Road'; the onions, pine trees and springs in 'Green Onions'; the kiln in 'White Trousers', and just retribution in 'The Shopkeeper'. In these stories, the peasants achieve some victory. But this is no false heroism, for Kemal seems to be aware that to imbue his peasants with undeserved heroism is to condescend towards them, to despise them, to reduce their humanity in an effort that would turn them into mere items in a moral or political debate. Kemal strenuously avoids the kind of heroism that scores points without being, at the same time, a celebration of achieved triumph. In the shorter stories, therefore, we are left with a hope that makes us contemplate the validity and worthiness of those moments in life that are joyful: that affirm it.

III

I became aware, after I had read Kemal's stories, that I did not remember ever coming across as compelling a body of fiction about peasant life in South Africa. It then seemed to me that there existed a disturbing silence in South African literature as far as peasants, as subjects of artistic attention, were concerned. There have, of course, been stories here and there. A lot of fiction in the African languages, Zulu or Sesotho, for example, is set in the rural areas. But almost invariably, the setting soon shifts to the towns; or, if not, the writers, armed with Christian zealousness, are merely concerned with eradicating 'superstition'. Seldom do we see peasants, *in their own right*, struggling to survive against the harsh conditions of nature or man-made injustice. What seems to be lacking, then, is an attempt at a sincere imaginative perception that sees South African peasant life as having a certain human validity, albeit a problematic one.

I became aware also, that much exciting and revealing research has been, and continues to be carried out on South African peasants by a recent crop of radical historians. Much of their work has been published by Ravan Press. But, with few exceptions, their research, and the discussions of it, appear to have been confined to the white liberal universities. Nevertheless, there has been no corresponding surge of interest in peasant subjects in our writers and artists: at least none that I am aware of. I cannot exactly make up my mind about the reasons for both the silence and for the lack of interest in response to the scholarly efforts; but I shall tentatively suggest a few.

Firstly, as far as the possible response to scholarly research is concerned, we have here yet another glaring tragedy of South African life. For historical reasons, it is mainly the whites who have access to the best educational facilities. This means that any research of radical interest which, by definition, has to emanate from, and its evaluation be situated in, the very current of the African struggle as it evolves, has no organic relationship with that struggle. So it cannot enrich the struggle in the *immediate* instance. This is so from the perspective of information giving as well as the assimilation of that information. Michael Vaughan, in a recent issue of *English in Africa*, makes the following observation which is most pertinent to what I'm saying:

> As one white academic critic, I have certainly felt myself drawn more and more to the position that most socially significant developments in literature in South Africa are taking place in black township literature. To engage with this developing literature in a social-critical spirit has come to represent an

absolute critical priority. At the same time, this engagement raises the question of critical 'address'. Black township literature is written by and for the inhabitants of black townships: its concepts, and the criticism and self-criticism that sustain and correct it are derived largely from the ideological and political milieu of the township – a milieu I do not share, except in the form of certain texts, which, furthermore, come to me divorced from their normative contextual associations.[5]

He then states, in what could easily apply to historical research, that 'academic criticism of contemporary black literature must be extremely circumscribed in its practice so long as it is deprived of contact with the writers and public of this literature'.[6] It would seem to follow then, that African fiction in South Africa would stand to benefit qualitatively if and when a radical intellectual tradition was to be effectively placed in and developed from the ranks of the mass struggle. It is there that the writers will also inevitably be found.

Secondly, the city appears to have taken tyrannical hold on the imagination of the average African writer. The situation, no doubt, has historical roots. The South African industrial revolution occasioned a massive flow of labour from the rural areas into the towns and cities of the country. Once there, those Africans who managed to acquire an education did not have any material or compelling ideological incentives to return to their peasant origins, neither physically nor imaginatively. We are now talking not of individuals here and there who return, but of socially significant movements. So, peasant consciousness never seriously benefited from the now relatively sophisticated intellectual perspectives of its own original sons and daughters. The 'Jim comes to Jo'burg' theme was the only viable compromise. In time, Jim sank his roots firmly in Jo'burg and encouraged a tendency which validated only the city experience as worthy of artistic attention. The setting had to be Johannesburg, then Cape Town, then Durban, then . . . in descending order of importance. In effect, life outside of the major urban centres was all but obliterated. Only the miners would oftentimes be an irritating reminder, as Nat Nakasa observed.[7]

Thirdly, the perception appears to have consolidated within the ranks of the liberation struggle that the decisive element in determining the course of the coming South African future, is the workers in the cities. That might be so, and is theoretically understandable. But what of the millions of Africans in the rural areas who, at that very decisive moment, might decide the fate of the hinterland? What of the deliberate peasantisation of urban Africans by the government through the Bantustans? The peasant position within the economic and political structures that govern the organic relationship between the urban and rural social formations might be theoretically understandable. But the peasant's *actual* aspirations, it seems, are a matter that ought not to be taken for granted.

Whatever the reasons, it does look as if, both from the political and the cultural perspectives, an important dimension has been left out of the total South African experience as that experience attempts to be conscious of itself and to define itself. However, one can predict the coming, in the not too distant future, of an era of urban obsession with rural areas as genuine sources of an array of cultural symbols by which to define a future cultural dispensation in South Africa. In a sense, that era has already begun. When it is running full steam ahead, that era will come with declarations asserting the need for an awareness of tradition that goes back into a peasant past. The era will doubtlessly idealise that past, thus defeating its own intentions. Perhaps the time is now in which to make a calm and objective reassessment.

One thing is clear, though. We are in the cities, anyhow, so what is the state of writing there?

In general, writers in the cities seem to be clear about one thing: that their writings should show, of themselves and their writers, a commitment to political engagement. According to this view, a poem or a work of fiction should most decidedly be written and be read

13

as offering necessary political insights. It should 'strike a blow for freedom'. Now, while most writers can agree on this aim, they may not necessarily have the same thing in mind about what implications this agreement has for the actual relationship between art and society; or, more specifically, between art and politics. The central problem here appears to lie in the often confusing paradox that art is an autonomous entity which, at the same time, derives its objective validity from and within society. This latter condition would then, by definition, appear to deny artistic autonomy. Something there is, therefore, in art that determines its autonomy; and something there is that appears necessarily to undercut that autonomy. Writers might therefore fall into two camps: according to whether they emphasise what makes for artistic autonomy, on the one hand; or, on the other hand, according to whether they emphasise the undercutting elements. It is the latter camp that is often easily defined as 'engaged' or 'committed' or 'relevant'.

What so readily seems to undercut the autonomy of art is its subject matter: the specificity of setting, the familiarity of character, recognisable events in either recent or distant history, and other similar factors that ground a work firmly in time and space. In societies such as South Africa, where social, economic, and political oppression is stark, such conditions tend to enforce, almost with the power of natural law, overt tendentiousness in the artist's choice of subject matter, and in the handling of that subject matter. It is such tendentiousness which, because it can most easily be interpreted as 'taking a position', earns a work of art the title of 'commitment' or 'engagement'. Clearly then, according to this attitude, artistic merit or relevance is determined less by a work's internal coherence (a decisive principle for autonomy) than by the work's displaying a high level of explicit political pre-occupation which may not necessarily be critically aware of the demands of the artistic medium chosen.

If the average South African writer has chosen this kind of preoccupation, what effect has it had on his or her writing? One major effect is that the writing's probing into the South African experience has been largely superficial. This superficiality comes from the tendency to produce fiction that is built around the interaction of surface symbols of the South African reality. These symbols can easily be characterised of either good or evil, or, even more accurately, symbols of evil on the one hand, and symbols of the victims of evil on the other hand. Thus, as far as the former symbols are concerned, we shall find an array of 'sell-outs', '*baases*', 'madams', policemen, cruel farmers and their overseers, Bantustans, farm labour, township superintendents and their subordinate functionaries. On the other hand, the victims will be *tsotsis*, convicts, beggars, washerwomen, road-gang labourers, night-watchmen, priests, shebeen kings and queens, and various kinds of 'law-abiding' citizens. All these symbols appear in most of our writings as finished products, often without a personal history. As such they appear as mere ideas to be marshalled this way or that in a moral debate. Their human anonymity becomes the dialectical equivalent of the anonymity to which the oppressive system consigns millions of oppressed Africans. Thus, instead of clarifying the tragic human experience of oppression, such fiction becomes grounded in the very negation it seeks to transcend.

The problem is that this kind of fiction is almost certainly the product of an ideology whose analysis of society is based on moral premises. In this view, the problems of South Africa are premised on the moral evil of apartheid. The major commitment of such a moral ideology is the *exposure* of the existence of social evil with the aim of pricking the human conscience of those responsible for that evil. The result is not knowledge but indictment; and indictment, because it assumes an accusatory stance, evokes a defensive attitude which may prevent the oppressor from reforming the system. He may even attempt to consolidate the system thus proving the indictment against it false. All this is because moral ideology tends to ossify complex social problems into symbols which are perceived as finished forms of good or evil, instead of leading us towards important necessary insights into the social *processes* leading to those finished forms. Thus, showing no more than surfaces, writings influenced by such an ideology tend to *inform* without involving readers in a truly transforming experience.

Indeed, the problem of *information* in a modern capitalist society appears to be at the root of the matter. (It is not too long ago that South Africa had what was called the 'Information Scandal'.) The issue is that indictment, by its very nature, requires *information* in order to be validated. And the more dramatic the information, and the more strikingly perfect it is in its finished form as a symbol of the devastating effects of apartheid, then the more desirable it is as a weapon of moral war. Thus, the writer of indictment soon gives himself or herself up to dealing with the oppressive negation on its own terms. And these terms, at their starkest, are numbing sensationalism and its consequent smothering of creative thinking. What we have is a conflict between the aim of storytelling and that of imparting social information. It is at this point that a competition between creative writing and journalism ensues. Lewis Nkosi's criticism of this 'competition' is well known.[8] In fact, it is not accurate to describe this relationship as a competitive one. Rather, what we have is creative writing's almost obsessive emulation of journalism. But Lewis Nkosi did not go far enough in his analysis of the problem.

The phenomenon of information in a capitalist society hinges on such issues as who produces the information, who interprets it, and who disseminates it. Now, to the average African writer in South Africa (invariably placed in opposition to the government by virtue of race, colour, economic and political status) the production, interpretation, and dissemination of information by the South African government and its agencies renders such information suspect. On the other hand, information produced, interpreted and disseminated by a variety of liberal institutions tends to be more readily accepted because such institutions are perceived to be morally opposed to government policy on matters of race relations. This acceptance, in the evolution of African political resistance, has over the years, almost become dependence. And this dependence was almost unavoidable. The liberal institutions of higher learning, liberal research agencies, and liberal press, by pouring out masses of information on the iniquities of apartheid, have dominated the information giving activity for the general opposition.

Furthermore, the liberal institutions' essentially anthropological approach gradually consolidated a picture of African society under South African oppression as a debased society. Studies and press reports on *tsotsi* violence, shebeens, convicts, sexual promiscuity, faction fighting, mine compound life, 'witchdoctors', 'strange' African customs and other instances of pathetic suffering have determined public (both black and white) perceptions of African suffering under apartheid. On the other hand, African medical doctors, teachers, township musicians, lawyers and others have been condescendingly promoted as symbols of African progress. But such promotional activity produced its opposite effect; the reinforcement of the image of debasement, because these figures were perceived as caricatures of sophisticated white men. Needless to say, all these images were highly marketable ones, and the press did its duty in consolidating stereotypes and prejudices. In African newspapers advertising promoted corresponding commodities of debasement: liquor, skin lightening creams, high-tar tobacco on the one hand, and correspondence schools, etc on the other hand, playing on eager hopes.

One can possibly assert with some confidence, then, that the average literate African's perception and conceptualisation of the African predicament in South Africa has been fashioned by the white liberal establishment. For example, the popularity of the *Daily Mail* and its influence in the townships over the years should always be understood within the context of the newspaper's link with Anglo American, which in turn has more than casual links with such institutions of higher learning as the University of the Witwaters-rand, and such liberal research agencies as the Institute of Race Relations, all of which belong to a specific ideological climate.

It can be surmised then, that in general the African resistance movement has not been in control of the information gathering, interpretation, and dissemination process. Under such conditions it is easy for sloganeering, defined as superficial thinking, to develop. The psychology of the slogan in these circumstances is the psychology of intellectual powerlessness. For example, the constant reference to the terrible South African Establishment as fascist, racist, imperialist, satanic, etc., while true, becomes mere verbal evocation acting as a façade for what might appear to be an empty desperate intellectual centre lacking in firmly established traditions of intellectual rigour. The slogan is the substitution of the gut response for clarity of analysis based on systematically acquired information. Those who have not domesticated the information gathering process at the institutional level are doomed to receive information, even about themselves, second-hand. It will be argued, of course, that Africans *do* have information about themselves as the actual sufferers. That is so. But such information has only biological validity. Only institutionalised information is subject to ideological scrutiny. Unfortunately there has not been, among Africans, a consistently original intellectual and analytical base from which to domesticate information and turn it into a truly transforming tool of liberation.

Now, it is at the level of slogans that the resistance movement has traditionally turned away from the liberal establishment, in order to marshal the second-hand information against Afrikaner political power. The resulting conflict has a dimension to it that can most clearly be seen as a clash of slogans. It might be wondered why the Afrikaner resorts to slogans when he has his own information gathering, interpretation, and dissemination agencies. One possible answer is that the intellectual tradition of the Afrikaner must surely be based, with few exceptions, on one of the most profound traditions of rationalisations ever conceived, for surely they must see the evil of their own creation. It is at the point of this recognition that their own slogans begin. The purpose of Rhoodie's information agency was precisely to market oppression through attractive packages of slogans. In this situation, it is easy to see how the marketing of oppression through the various state agencies produces its dialectical opposite: the 'marketing' of resistance. In this conflict, the slogan of oppression qualitatively equals the slogan of resistance.

18

Both are verbal claims making little attempt to genuinely involve the 'consumers' as equals in the quest for truth.

What implications has all this had for creative writing? It should be clear. I once met a writer who gleefully told me how honoured he felt that his book of poetry had been banned by the South African censors. What I found disturbing was the ease with which the writer ascribed some kind of heroism to himself, almost glorying in a negation. It did not occur to him, of course, that the censors may have banned his work precisely because they may have seen in it their own 'games', their own tactics, their own quality of propaganda, their own vindictiveness, their own debasement. The writer may have concentrated on those aspects of social reality and the methods of treating that reality which interest the censors to the extent that the censors cannot think beyond them. The censor may have seen not experience, but social information that simply conflicted with his own. The whole problem, of course, might be more complex than that. I was merely trying to challenge what seemed to be a dangerously complacent attitude.

The truth is that the average African writer, working under an information ethos which for him has not habituated a tradition of rigorous analysis and interpretation, produces an art of anticipated surfaces rather than one of processes: processes in character development or in social evolution, for example. He produces an art that is grounded in the negation of social debasement, where scenes of social violence and a host of examples of general social oppression become ends in themselves. As a result very little transformation in reader consciousness is to be expected since the only reader faculty engaged is the faculty of recognition. Recognition does not necessarily lead to transformation: it simply confirms. Beyond that confirmation, it may even reinforce the frustration produced by the reader's now further consolidated perception of an overwhelmingly negative social reality.

For example, it will be recalled that it was the aesthetics of recognition that was the basis of dissatisfaction with the early poetry of Oswald Mtshali. I have also found Mtutuzeli Matshoba's depiction of social reality in his stories simply too overwhelming. His basic technique has been to accumulate fact after fact of oppression and suffering, so that we are in the end almost totally grounded in this reality without being offered, at the same time, an opportunity for aesthetic and critical estrangement. Recently, Mbulelo Mzamane has produced a novel, *The Children of Soweto*, grounded almost entirely in the events of June 16, 1976. I found no independent narrative line that permits any reader involvement beyond the act of recognition. On the contrary Sipho Sepamla's *A Ride on the Whirlwind* has an independent plot line. An African guerrilla fighter has sneaked back into South Africa on a mission to kill. His arrival coincides with the events of June 16, 1976. It is this existence of a plot line that makes Sepamla's novel more narratively engaging than Mzamane's. In his novel Sepamla constantly struggles to subject the objective events to the demands of his art. He does not entirely succeed, but he is moving in the right direction. Where lies the possible remedy, then?

Basically, the demands of the craft of fiction are that a writer has to have a more than casual view of the relationship between fiction and society, or between artistic information and social information. The world of fiction demands that the writer grapple with some of the following problems which are basic to his art: setting, conflict, credible characterisation, consistent narrative point of view, the complexities of fictional language and time. Beyond these essential technical issues, a serious writer must address himself to the ideological nature of fiction, since the handling of social information, whether within the narrative, or within ordinary discourse, is always ideologically determined. The moralistic ideology of liberalism for example, has forced our literature into a tradition of almost mechanistic surface representation. On the other hand, an ideological stance which stresses social or historical process as a condition for the meaningful acquisition of knowledge will more easily dispose writers towards a more explanatory approach to fiction. To work from the perspective of process is to attempt to situate individual events within an explainable totality of social meaning.

The example of character development may serve to shed some light on what I am trying to say. In a critical appreciation of Mtutuzeli Matshoba's stories (*Staffrider*, Vol.4, No.3), Michael Vaughan observes that in Matshoba's work 'the whole liberal preoccupation with the individual interiority, and hence with subtle and elaborate characterisation, is dispensed with. Characterisation establishes individual specificity and separateness, a function which is not relevant to Matshoba's project.' It seems clear that Vaughan's position with regard to liberal philosophy is critical. On this basis, although he does not say so explicitly, Vaughan implies that a writer's concern with subjectivity in character development may amount to a bourgeois or liberal escapism into an ethos of individualism. But is that necessarily so?

Herbert Marcuse's views on the question of subjectivity in bourgeois culture are too persuasive to be easily dispensed with. He notes that:

> even in bourgeois society, insistence on the truth and right of inwardness is not really a bourgeois value. With the affirmation of the inwardness of subjectivity, the individual steps out of the network of exchange relationships and exchange values, withdraws from the reality of bourgeois society, and enters another dimension of existence. Indeed, this escape from reality led to an experience which could (and did) become a powerful force in invalidating the actual prevailing bourgeois values, namely by shifting the locus of the individual's realisation from the domain of the performance principle and the profit motive to that of the inner resources of the human being: passion, imagination, conscience. Moreover, withdrawal and retreat were not the last position. Subjectivity strove to break out of its inwardness into the material and intellectual culture. And today, in the totalitarian period, it has become a political value as a counterforce against aggressive and exploitative socialisation.[9]

The point, therefore, is not to avoid interiority, but to render it *as concretely as possible* within the unfolding logic of narrative.

As I am writing this essay, I happen to be reading Graham Greene's *The Power and the Glory*, and I have only just finished a chapter which begins in the following manner:

> The mule suddenly sat down under the priest. It was not an unnatural thing to do, for they had been travelling through the forest for nearly twelve hours. They had been going west, but news of soldiers met them there and they had turned east; the Red Shirts were active in that direction, so they had tacked north, wading through swamps, diving into the mahogany darkness. Now they were both tired out and the mule simply sat down. The priest scrambled off and began to laugh. He was feeling happy. It is one of the strange discoveries a man can make that life, however you lead it, contains moments of exhilaration; there are always comparisons which can be made with worse times: even in danger and misery the pendulum swings.[10]

Here is a man during a moment of insightful intimacy with himself; a moment of transcendence. Most wonderful in this little piece of narrative is how it makes subtle shifts in narrative point of view: how it is now outside and objective ('the mule suddenly sat down under the priest'), and now it is inside and subjective ('it was not an unnatural thing to do'). The latter is an evaluative statement that can only spring from inner reflection projected onto the animal. In a subtle manner, we are let into the subjective life of the priest through a deceptively objective narrative stance. The picture suggested of the priest is that of a sympathetic man, grateful of the role of his mule in getting him out of danger. The priest is deeply relieved that his keen sense of self-preservation had led him to safety. Seen in this perspective, the laughter of the priest is far from irrational. It represents a triumphant moment of inner realisation, triggered off by the sense of the priest's having momentarily overcome objective danger and finding himself in a moment of deserved celebration. Such moments are not an escape into bourgeois fantasy. On the contrary, they are a universal experience, and because we recognise them as such whenever we see them, we are, in this case, led into a sympathetic pact with the priest. Here is what I mean by interiority concretely rendered.

It seems clear, therefore, that it is humanly unrealistic to show a revolutionary hero, for example, who has no inner doubts. All great revolutionaries from Lenin, through Nkrumah, to Ché Guevara, among others, have had to grapple with inner fears, anxieties, and doubts. In appreciating this fact, one gains an insight into the human reality of their heroism. A reader confronted with such heroism, experiences himself as potentially capable of it too, if only he could learn to find a way of dealing with his fears.

'The need for radical change,' asserts Marcuse, 'must be rooted in the subjectivity of individuals themselves, in their intelligence and their passions, their drives and their goals.'[11] The specific subjectivity of character is universalised through the reader's recognition of familiar emotions generated in a given event. Thus, a reader, confronted with a *dramatisation of process* in character development, grows with the story.

Perhaps more light can be thrown on this issue if one considers the problem of the villain in a story. This is particularly pertinent to the problem of portraying functionaries of the oppressive system in South Africa: the 'mayors', 'presidents' of 'independent states', policemen, informers, etc. Is it useful, in the quest for a transforming social understanding, for a writer always to portray such characters as finished products: unaccountably vicious, cruel, malicious, fawning and greedy? Obviously not. And here, the maturity of the writer is called for, since he is called upon to be fair-minded even to those he socially abhors. The point is that attempting to understand the villain in all his complexity does not necessarily imply a political acceptance of him. On the contrary, it may intensify political opposition even more. Artistic compassion only situates the villain within the domain of tragic acceptance, which, in practice, translates itself into moral or political rejection. We cannot wish away evil; but genuine art makes us understand it. Only then can we purposefully deal with it.

Returning to Vaughan's discussion of Matshoba's characterisation, one would note that where the demand for a surface art emanates from within the radical intellectual movement, it becomes the dialectical opposite of the demonstrative liberal approach already seen above. It represents no qualitative improvement. On the contrary, it manages to become a liberalisation of the practice of radical dialectical thinking by appearing to give political morality an all too ready precedence over inclusive and liberating understanding.

Finally, I want to refer to an interesting interview of Miriam Tlali, Sipho Sepamla, and Mothobi Mutloatse, by Jaki Seroke (*Staffrider*, Vol.4, No.3), in which at least two issues of interest to me are raised. Firstly, Mothobi Mutloatse criticises the press for being 'so sweeping in its criticism of the new wave of black writing. They say it is too obviously political; it cannot offer anything else. We see the new writing as part of what is happening. It is a type of writing that *is perfectly suited to the times*. We need a writing that records exactly the situation we live in, and any writing which *ignores the urgency of political events will be irrelevant*' [emphasis mine]. One might ask: in what way is writing 'perfectly suited to the times'? In what way does writing 'record exactly the situation we live in'? What kind of writing emerging at the same time as the writing that fulfils Mutloatse's conditions, is deemed to ignore 'the urgency of political events', thus rendering itself 'irrelevant', even possibly, irrespective of the seriousness of its intention? These questions raise serious critical questions the answers to which ought not to be complacently taken for granted. And, in addressing those questions, we may need to make a distinction between the *journalistic*, informational ambience on the one hand, and the *storytelling*, narrative ambience on the other.

For example, Miriam Tlali complains that she has been accused of speaking 'about the matters just as they are instead of building them into the emotions of the reader. As if it's just reporting'. But why is the parting scene at the end of Tlali's novel, *Amandla*, so effective? It's because the hero and his girl *are in love*. Any situation that forces lovers apart will invite our condemnation. Now, the vast majority of people, I think, enjoy reading about lovers. Almost all of us are, or were, or will be lovers. Thus, we feel with Tlali's lovers, we can identify with their problem. What Tlali has done is build into her characters 'the emotions of the reader': the very thing which Tlali, in this interview, appears not to want her work to be associated with. Clearly, the artist in her repudiates the critic in her. In any case, *Amandla* is, in my opinion, the best of the novels written on the events of June 16, 1976. It surpasses, in the quality of its art, Sepamla's *A Ride on the Whirlwind*, and Mzamane's *Children of Soweto*. Tlali was not 'just reporting', she was telling a story.

When Sipho Sepamla in the interview agrees with Miriam Tlali that 'we have to go to the people', for 'it is the man in the street that I feel we must listen to', he is probably establishing the premise on which is based one fundamental assumption shared by all three writers: that the 'political' writers are writing what the African masses really want. Is that assumption a valid one? When Sepamla listens to 'the man in the street' what does he hear? I have listened to countless storytellers on the buses and trains carrying people to and from work in South Africa. The majority of them have woven master-pieces of entertainment and instruction. Others were so popular that commuters made sure they did not miss the storyteller's trains. The vast majority of the stories were either tragedies or comedies about lovers, township jealousies, the worries of widows; about the need to consult medicine men for luck at horse racing, or luck at getting a job or at winning a football match; or they were fantastic ghost stories (let's remember here Bheki Maseko's 'Mamlambo', *Staffrider*, Vol.5, No.1; here is a writer who has listened to the man in the street, and heard); they have woven satires about the assassination of Verwoerd by Tsafendas (if you threatened to stab someone those days you could say, 'I will tsafenda you'); they have woven stories about helicopter weddings, about African soldiers seeing ships, the sea and Europe for the first time in World War II. And we have to face the truth here: there were proportionately fewer overtly political stories. When they talked politics, they talked politics; when they told stories, they told stories. If any political concept crept into the stories, it was domesticated by a fundamental interest in the evocation of the general quality of African life in the township. Where is the concept of 'relevance' here?

When we turn to the lyrics of the vast majority of popular songs in 'soul' and *mbaqanga* music, we find a similar situation: lyrics about infidelity, about the relationships between women and their in-laws, about the problem of going to work early in the morning, about weddings, about the joys of music. As I am writing, a new hit is ringing in my mind. The lyrics tell school children to heed the school bell summoning them to go and learn how to read, write, count, and sing. Then I am reminded of Thamsanqa's story 'Have You Seen Sticks?' (*Staffrider*, Vol.4, No.3), and then the entire African experience of going to school in South Africa is laid bare before me, accompanied by an exhilaration emerging from my having been given the opportunity to recall, to reflect and to evaluate a common experience in all the townships of South Africa; indeed, the world over.

In all these stories and songs, I am made conscious of Africans in South Africa as makers of culture in their own right. I am made conscious of them as philosophers, asking ultimate questions about life, moral values, and social being. And I am forced to conclude that if the conscious political will does not embrace this totality, it is bound to come out with a skewed vision of the future. I am aware too, that we do have novels which address themselves to this totality: Dikobe's *Marabi Dance*; Nyembezi's *Inkisela Yase Mgugundlovu*; Mofolo's *Chaka*; Jordan's *Ingqambo Yeminyanya*; Boetie's *Familarity is the Kingdom of the Lost*; Mphahlele's *In Corner B*; and more recently, the stories of Joël Matlou and Bheki Maseko in *Staffrider*. What is common to these writers is that they are storytellers, not just case makers. They give African readers the opportunity to experience themselves as makers of culture. They make it possible for people to realise that in the making of culture, even those elements of life that are seen not to be *explicitly* oriented to resistance, are valid. Indeed, the latter may upon reflection (crucial to the under-cutting of the ethos of the market place) be found to represent a much wider, and richer, because more inclusive, context of resistance. The matter is simple: there is a difference between art that 'sells' ideas to the people, and that in which ideas are *embraced* by the people, because they have been made to understand them through the evocation of lived experience in all its complexities. In the former case, the readers are anonymous buyers; in the latter, they are equals in the quest for truth. All the writer needs to understand is that he can only be genuinely committed to politics through a commitment to the demands of his art.

There is one other thing that emerges from the *Staffrider* interview. There appears to be a rather disturbing anti-intellectual attitude in Sepamla and Tlali with regard to the practice of literary criticism. We have just seen above how Tlali's artistic practice contradicts her own critical assertions. She continues later: 'Writing is an art like all the other forms and it should not be pipelined or squeezed in a water-tight channel.' Isn't this what the critics are in fact saying? They couldn't agree more, for they perceive the literary situation to be narrow-minded and 'pipelined or squeezed' in its artistic ori-entation. It seems to me that Miriam Tlali may not have thought out the implications of her own artistic practice fully and carefully, and all too readily dismisses the critic who, if he is serious and genuine, might *legitimately* raise issues that may clarify her own position.

About readers and critics, Miriam Tlali declares: 'It is the reader who must judge, not these masters of literature.' One might ask: are critics not readers too? Of course, what she means is that she prefers the judgement of the enthusiastically uncritical average reader (she is after all one up on them – she spent much thought in composing her novels), to the judgement of one who may have painstakingly spent much thought in trying to *understand* her work. I do not believe that is what she really desires, for she goes on to say: 'It is quite a task to write. In the first place you have to be fortunate enough to have an education which can enable you to express yourself.' Although Tlali accepts the importance of education, she does not go far enough. One result of education is heightened, critical awareness which will not shy away from applying that awareness to literature. Surely this is what she wants!

Furthermore, Tlali is surely correct in complaining that 'so-called critics labour under a misconception in that they say that in order to write you have to be a literary scholar'. A writer does not have to be a literary scholar in the academic sense. But then, it is useful to note what Henry James has to say on the issue. 'There is,' he says, 'one point at which the moral sense and the artistic sense lie very near together: that is in the light of the very obvious truth that the deepest quality of a work of art will always be the quality of the mind of the producer. In proportion as that intelligence is fine will the novel, the picture, the statue partake of the substance of beauty and truth.'[12] At the root of this sentiment is the requirement that since the world and the people on it are the writer's business, he has constantly to enlarge his intellectual horizons regarding his key focus. There seems no escape from this necessity.

Sepamla echoes Tlali on the question of critics: 'Instead of encouraging a person who is making an attempt we try to destroy this person. What we hope to gain mystifies me. There is nothing that a so-called critic will gain by destroying this book. Instead he will prevent the black people from making progress.' Sepamla goes on to lament the fact that 'some of these critics are Black Consciousness adherents'. Firstly, there is a danger here that critics might be accused of being unpatriotic simply because we do not agree with what they say. Secondly, does it mean that 'Black Consciousness adherents' must uncritically rave enthusiastically about anything written by blacks? Nothing could be more dangerous to the struggle than the suppression of criticism. The two attitudes above are not only anti-intellectual, they are also essentially undemocratic. If we want to struggle towards a genuinely democratic future, then we must be prepared to subject *everything* to rigorous intellectual scrutiny followed by open and fearless discussion. Writers and critics can make their contribution too. The demands made on us by the future leave no room in which to feel sorry for ourselves.

We have come a long way from Turkish tales. The thoughts they have triggered no doubt need further discussion. I could not at this stage go beyond a preliminary identification and statement of key problems. The Turkish tales, I believe, contain the essence of what is universal in the art of narrative. My attention was then necessarily turned home, where I believe we should produce works that will not only inspire us through the enchanting powers of art, but will also be embraced well beyond our borders as a joyful lesson.

NOTES

1. Yashar Kemal, *Anatolian Tales,* (London: Writers and Readers, 1983).
2. See Walter Benjamin, 'The Storyteller', in *Illuminations*, Harry Zohn (trans.), (London: Jonathan Cape, 1970).
3. Walter Benjamin, p.84.
4. Andrew Mango, *Turkey,* (London: Thames & Hudson, 1983), pp.122–3.
5. Michael Vaughan, 'Ideological Directions in the Study of Southern African Literature'. *English in Africa*, Vol.9, No.2, 1982, p.62.
6. Michael Vaughan, p.63.
7. Nat Nakasa, 'Johannesburg Johannesburg'. *The Classic*, Vol.2, No.1, 1966, p.19.
8. Lewis Nkosi, 'Fiction by Black South Africans', in *Introduction to African Literature*, Ulli Beier (ed.), (London: Longman, 1967), p.222.
9. Herbert Marcuse, *The Aesthetic Dimension: Toward a Critique of Marxist Aesthetics*, (Boston: Beacon Press, 1978), pp.4–5.
10. Graham Greene, *The Power and the Glory*, (U.K.: Penguin Books, 1962), p.59.
11. Herbert Marcuse, p.3.
12. Henry James, *The House of Fiction*, L. Edel (ed.), (London: Rupert Hart-Davis, 1975), p.44.

2

❖ ❖ ❖

THE REDISCOVERY OF THE ORDINARY:
SOME NEW WRITINGS IN SOUTH AFRICA

The history of black South African literature has largely been the history of the representation of spectacle. The visible symbols of the overwhelmingly oppressive South African social formation appear to have prompted over the years the development of a highly dramatic, highly demonstrative form of literary representation. One is reminded here of Roland Barthes's essay on wrestling. Some of Barthes's observations on the wrestling match seem particularly apposite.[1] 'The virtue of all-in wrestling,' Barthes opens his essay, 'is that it is the spectacle of excess.'[2] It is the manifest display of violence and brutality that captures the imaginations of the spectators. Indeed, we have seen the highly organised spectacle of the political wrestling match of the South African social formation. Everything in South Africa has been mind-bogglingly spectacular: the monstrous war machine developed over the years; the random massive pass raids; mass shootings and killings; mass economic exploitation the ultimate symbol of which is the mining industry; the mass removals of people; the spate of draconian laws passed with the spectacle of parliamentary promulgations; the luxurious life-style of whites:

This paper was presented as the keynote address at the conference on *New Writing in Africa: Continuity and Change* held at the Commonwealth Institute, London, November 1984.

servants, all encompassing privilege, swimming pools, and high commodity consumption; the sprawling monotony of architecture in African locations, which are the very picture of poverty and oppression. The symbols are all over: the quintessence of obscene social exhibitionism. And at the centre of it all, are the main actors: the aggressive Boer who has taken three centuries to develop the characteristics of the massive wrestler. It could be said, therefore, that the most outstanding feature of South African oppression is its brazen, exhibitionist openness.

It is no wonder then, that the black writer, sometimes a direct victim, sometimes a spectator, should have his imagination almost totally engaged by the spectacle before him.

T.T. Moyana must have had this situation in mind when he pointed to the problematic relationship between art and objective reality in South Africa:

> An additional difficulty for the creative artist in South Africa, especially the black writer, is that life itself is too fantastic to be outstripped by the creative imagination. Nkosi calls the theme of the absurd the theme of daily living in South. Indeed, many writers of the absurd school would find their plots too realistic to startle anybody into serious questioning of their deeper meaning. How would the quarrel over a bench in Edward Albee's *Zoo Story* startle anybody in a country where thousands of people have been daily quarrelling over who should sit on a particular park bench, and the country's parliament has had legislation on the matter? That's much more startling than Albee's little quarrel between two men. And Kafka himself would not have bettered the case told by Lewis Nkosi. He was arrested by a policeman who then phoned his superior to ask, 'What shall I charge him with?' Or the incident of a white man and a coloured woman who were tried for being caught kissing. The court got bogged down over the question of whether the kiss was 'platonic or passionate'. One reporter who covered the case for a local

newspaper wrote: 'Lawyers and laymen are certain that the Minister of Justice will now have to consider an amendment to the law which will define the various degrees of kissing from the platonic to the passionate'.[3]

What is on display here is the spectacle of social absurdity. The necessary ingredients of this display are precisely the triteness and barrenness of thought, the almost deliberate waste of intellectual energy on trivialities. It is, in fact, the 'emptying out of interiority to the benefit of its exterior signs, (the) exhaustion of the content by the form'.[4] The overwhelming form is the method of displaying the culture of oppression to the utmost in bewilderment.

A very brief review of black South African writing in English will reveal the glaring history of spectacular representation. The stories of R.R.R. Dhlomo, for example, are characterised by tightness of plot, emphasis on the most essential items of plot, the predominance of dialogue, and sudden, almost unexpected shocking endings, all of which are the ingredients of dramatic writing.[5] Dhlomo is interested only in the outward, obvious signs of individual or social behaviour. Causality is a matter of making simple connections in order to produce the most startling and shocking results. There is very little attempt to delve into intricacies of motive or social process. People and situations are either very good or very bad. Those who are bad, invariably abandon their evil ways overnight. And so, Dhlomo takes us, in this highly dramatic manner, through the working conditions in the mines, through the physical and moral squalor of Prospect Township, and through the sophisticated domestic life of young African couples playing with the game of love.

In *Drum Magazine*, we see a similar penchant for the spectacular, although the symbols are slightly different. It is not so much the symbols of oppression that we see in most of the stories in *Drum*, but those showing the growth of sophisticated urban working and petty-bourgeois classes. The literary ingredients for the dramatic in these stories are: pacey style, suspenseful plots with the unexpected ending, characters speaking like Americans, dressed like them, and driving American cars. Perhaps the detective story serials of Arthur

Mogale typify this kind of writing. Detective Morena is a self-made man, confident, fast talking, and quick thinking, playing the game of wits with his adversaries. He wins. Clearly, it is the spectacle of phenomenal social change and the growing confidence of the urban African population that we see being dramatised here.

It might be asked why the vast majority of these stories in *Drum* show an almost total lack of interest in the directly political issues of the time. After all, the Nationalists had just acquired power in 1948 and were busy 'putting the Kaffirs in their place'. The writers of these stories seemed keen only to tell fantastic stories so that readers could enjoy themselves as much as possible. They were pushed forward in their writings in order to indulge the lively imagination of the urban population. They reflected the tremendous energy that was generated in the urban areas of South Africa. But going hand-in-hand with these stories was a very lively journalism: the investigative journalism of Henry Nxumalo, for example, revealed much of the gross ugliness of economic exploitation in South Africa. The covering of strikes and political meetings was done in a highly spectacular journalistic fashion. There seemed no confusion at this time between the language of exposition on the one hand, and the language of creative writing on the other. Creative writers simply titillated the readers with good stories, and the journalists concentrated on their work, writing about politics, sports, fashion, etc. What was common though, was the penchant for spectacular representation or reporting. The thick lines of spectacle were drawn with obvious relish.

At the end of the fifties, and following the banning of the ANC and the PAC, we begin to see the emergence of what has been called Protest Literature. This kind of writing follows the disillusionment that came in the wake of the bannings of the major political organisations. Here we see the return to the concerns of Dhlomo. We see the dramatic politicisation of creative writing in which there is a movement away from the entertaining stories of *Drum*, towards stories revealing the spectacular ugliness of the South African situation in all its forms: the brutality of the Boer, the terrible farm conditions, the phenomenal hypocrisy of the English speaking liberal, the disillusionment of educated Africans, the poverty of African life, crime, and a host of other things. The bulk of the stories of James Matthews, Ezekiel Mphahlele, Alex La Guma, Can Themba, Webster Makaza, and others falls into this category.

Picking out a story at random, we shall find the firm outlines of this kind of writing. 'Coffee for the Road', a story by Alex La Guma, is about an Indian woman and her children driving through the Karoo on a long tiring journey to Cape Town. The strain of driving, and the lack of social amenities for blacks to provide rest along the way are described vividly by La Guma:

> The mother had been driving all night and she was fatigued, her eyes red, with the feeling of sand under the lids irritating the eyeballs. They had stopped for a short while along the road, the night before; parked in a gap off the road outside a small town. There had been nowhere to put up for the night: the hotels were for Whites only. In fact, only Whites lived in these towns and everybody else, except for servants, lived in tumbledown mud houses in the locations beyond. Besides, they did not know anybody in this part of the country.[6]

The glaring contrasts are put there before us together with the very *obvious* explanation for their existence. The similarity to another dramatic story is evident here: the heavily pregnant Mary being turned away from every inn until the baby Jesus was born in a simple manger. The difference is that in La Guma's story there is no relief for the woman and her children. But it is the ritualistic enactment and the drawing of significant meaning that is at the aesthetic centre of these two stories:

> The landscape ripped by, like a film being run backwards, red-brown, yellow-red, pink-red, all studded with sparse bushes and broken boulders. To the east a huge outcrop of rock strata rose abruptly from the arid earth, like a titanic wedge of purple-and-lavender-layered cake topped with

chocolate-coloured boulders. The car passed over a stretch of gravel road and the red dust boiled behind it, skimmed the brush beyond the edge of the road, flitting along as fast as the car.

The symbolic barrenness of the landscape cannot be missed. The travellers pass a 'group of crumbling huts, like scattered, broken cubes'; and 'in a hollow near the road' they see 'a bank of naked, dusty, brown children'. They see three black men trudging 'in single file along the roadside, looking ahead into some unknown future, wrapped in tattered dusty blankets, oblivious of the heat, their heads shaded by the ruins of felt hats'.

But finally, they have to stop at a white town 'Just some place in the Karoo' in order to refill their coffee flask. Ignoring a 'foot-square hole where non-whites were served', the Indian mother simply walks into a café on the white side. The description of the white woman behind the counter is done with spectacular relish:

> Behind the glass counter and a trio of soda fountains a broad, heavy woman in a green smock thumbed through a little stack of accounts, ignoring the group of dark faces pressing around the square hole in the side wall. She had a round-shouldered, thick body and reddish-complexioned face that looked as if it had been sand-blasted into its component parts: hard plains of cheeks and knobbly cheek-bones and a bony ridge of nose that separated twin pools of dull grey; and the mouth a bitter gash, cold and malevolent as a lizard's chapped and serrated pink crack.

The very picture of a female ogre! Her response to the Indian woman's request for coffee is equally dramatic:

> The crack opened and a screech came from it, harsh as the sound of metal rubbed against stone. 'Coffee? My Lord Jesus Christ!' the voice screeched. 'A bedamned coolie girl in here!' The eyes started in horror at the brown, tired, handsome Indian

face with its smart sun-glasses, and the city cut of the tan suit. 'Coolies, Kaffirs and Hottentots outside,' she screamed. 'Don't you bloody well know? And you talk *English*, too, hey?'

The response of the Indian woman is heroically sudden, unpremeditated and spectacularly proper in its justice:

> The mother stared at her, startled, and then somewhere inside her something went off, snapped like a tight-wound spring suddenly loose, jangling shrilly into action, and she cried out with disgust as her arm came up and the thermos flask hurled at the white woman.

At this point, it might be best to leave to the imagination of the reader what damage was inflicted on the white woman by the flask. But La Guma will not leave anything to imagination:

> The flask spun through the air and, before the woman behind the counter could ward it off, it struck her forehead above an eyebrow, bounced away, tinkling as the thin glass inside the metal cover shattered. The woman behind the counter screeched and clapped a hand to the bleeding gash over her eye, staggering back . . . The dark faces at the square hatch gasped. The dark woman turned and stalked from the café in a rage.

Victory or retribution? It is bound to be one of the two, spectacularly drawn. Indeed, retribution follows. The Indian woman does not get far for there is a road-block ahead:

> A small riot-van, a Land Rover, its windows and spot light screened with thick wire mesh, had been pulled up half-way across the road, and a dusty automobile parked opposite to it, forming a barrier with just a car-wide space between them. A policeman in khaki shirt, trousers and flat cap leaned against

the front fender of the automobile and held a Sten-gun across his thighs. Another man in khaki sat at the wheel of the car, and a third policeman stood by the gap, directing the traffic through after examining the drivers.

We see the travellers for the last time as they are escorted back to town, a police car in front and behind, for whatever retribution is to follow: 'You make trouble here then you got to pay for it.'

Everything in La Guma's story points to spectacle: the complete exteriority of everything: the dramatic contrasts all over the story, the lack of specificity of place and character so that we have spectacular ritual instantly turned into symbol, with instant meaning (no interpretation here is necessary: seeing is meaning), and the intensifying device of hyphenated adjectives. Is it germane to ask whether there ever can be such unaccountably terrible people as the white woman in the story, such unaccountably dignified women as the Indian woman, such barren landscape, such utter desolation? Where is causality? Such questions are irrelevant. Subtlety is avoided: what *is* intended is spectacular demonstration at all costs. What matters is what is seen. Thinking is secondary to seeing. Subtlety is secondary to obviousness. What is finally left and what is deeply etched in our minds is the spectacular contest between the powerless and the powerful. Most of the time the contest ends in horror and tragedy for the powerless. Sometimes there are victories, but they are always proportionally secondary to the massively demonstrated horror that has gone before.

It needs only be stated briefly that spectacular representation is not confined to fiction; it is there in painting and sculpture where we are most likely to see grotesque figures in all kinds of contortions indicative of agony. In poetry, it will suffice to quote some lines from Dennis Brutus's famous untitled poem:

> The sounds begin again;
> the siren in the night
> the thunder at the door
> the shriek of nerves in pain.

Then the keening crescendo
of faces split by pain
the wordless, endless wail
only the unfree know.[7]

Beyond that, we can find the culture of the spectacular in *mbaqanga* music, in free-style township dance and even in football, where spectacular display of individual talent is often more memorable, more enjoyable, and ultimately, even more desirable than the final score.

Much of this writing has been denounced as unartistic, crude, and too political. There was more politics in it than art. In defence of the writing, it was asserted that there was nothing wrong with politics in literature because everything in South Africa, anyway, is political.[8] Both positions, it seems to me, miss the mark. As far as the former position is concerned, Chinweizu, Jemie, and Madubuike have comprehensively documented how a powerful Eurocentric school of criticism of African Literature has imposed on the literature evaluations based on false assumptions.[9] Such assumptions never enabled the critics using them to understand the real nature of much of what African Literature was doing and what its methods were. The same goes for the criticism of what has come to be known as Protest Literature in South Africa.

Once we begin to see an artistic convention emerging, once we see a body of writing exhibiting similar characteristics, we must attempt to identify its origins, its methods of operation, and its *effective* audience. Such factors will establish the validity of the writing. The writing will validate itself in terms of its own primary conventions; in terms of its own emergent, complex system of aesthetics. The whole plain of aesthetics here involves the transformation of objective reality into conventional tropes which become the predominant means by which that objective reality is artistically ritualised. The aesthetic validity of this literature to its own readership lies precisely in the readers' recognition of the spectacular rendering of a familiar oppressive reality. We have seen the South African origins of this literature, we have also had a glimpse of its methods in La Guma's story, but what of its audience?

The question of the audience for this 'protest literature' is a problematic one. Conventional wisdom proclaims that the literature was premised on its supposed appeal to the conscience of the white oppressor: 'If the oppressor sees himself as evil, he will be revolted by his negative image, and will try to change.' Indeed, the class position of most of the writers, the publications in which their writings appeared, the levels of literacy in English among the African population would *objectively* point towards a white audience: an English speaking liberal one at that. But that audience, schooled under a Eurocentric literary tradition, was in turn, schooled to reject this literature 'meant' for them. They rejected both the methods of representation as well as the content. Where they yielded to accept the validity of the content, they emphasised the crudeness of the method. But what of the audience for whom this literature was not 'objectively' meant? What about the *effective* audience?

We are familiar with how in the days when South Africa still participated in world soccer international teams visited the country for games. We are familiar with the spectacle of how African fans always cheered the visiting team against the white South African side. It happened in rugby too. It seems reasonable to assume that, at least at the populist level, if all black South Africans could read this 'protest literature', they would naturally take sides much to their aesthetic delight. The Indian woman in La Guma's story would be cheered, while the white woman and the white policeman would be detested. The black audience in the story itself is described as having 'gasped', probably in shock. But I am also certain that this was the response of having witnessed the unexpected. Inwardly, they must have experienced a delightful thrill at this 'great spectacle of Suffering, Defeat, and Justice'.[10] To evoke this response, the literature works this way: the more the brutality of the system is dramatised, the better; the more exploitation is revealed and starkly dramatised, the better. The more the hypocrisy of liberals is revealed, the better. Anyone whose sensibility has not been fashioned by such conditions will find such spectacular dramatisation somewhat jarring. In the same way that western dancers of the waltz found African dancing 'primitive', the aesthetics of reading this literature, for the black reader, is the aesthetics of recognition, understanding, historical documentation, and indictment. All these go together. For the white audience, on the other hand, what has been called 'protest literature' can, to borrow from Brecht, be considered a spectacular 'alienation effect'; a literature that refuses to be enjoyed precisely because it challenges 'conventional' methods of literary representation, and that it painfully shows up the ogre to himself.

Why the misnomer 'protest'? The misnomer devalues the literature as art since 'protest' carries the implications of political *and* specifically *expository* declaration of dissent. The misnomer is obviously taken from the concept of 'politics of protest'. But this literature, while definitely labouring under the pressure of the expository intention, deliberately sets out to use conventions of fiction not of exposition. To call it 'protest literature' is to deny it any literary and artistic value: and those values are to be found in the phenomenon of the spectacle. On this basis, it should be clear why I said above that even those who have come in defence of this literature have fallen into the same trap. They defiantly said: if you accuse us of being political, hard luck, that's what our writing is going to be because that is what the conditions dictate. The fault is not so much in the statement itself, but in the assumption that the statement reinforces. It reinforces the expository intention without establishing its own evaluative literary grounds.

We can now summarise the characteristics of the spectacular in this context. The spectacular documents; it indicts implicitly; it is demonstrative, preferring exteriority to interiority; it keeps the larger issues of society in our minds, obliterating the details; it provokes identification through recognition and feeling rather than through observation and analytical thought; it calls for emotion rather than conviction; it establishes a vast sense of presence without offering intimate knowledge; it confirms without necessarily offering a challenge. It is the literature of the powerless identifying the key factor

41

responsible for their powerlessness. Nothing beyond this can be expected of it.

Every convention will outlive its validity. Judging from some of the new writing that has emerged recently from the South African townships, one can come to the conclusion that the convention of the spectacular has run its course. Its tendency either to devalue or to ignore interiority has placed it firmly in that aspect of South African society that constitutes its fundamental weakness. South African society, as we have seen, is a very public society. It is public precisely in the sense that its greatest aberrations are fully exhibited. One effect of this is the suppression of deep-rooted individuals as well as social fears. But not only fears are suppressed: the deepest dreams for love, hope, compassion, newness and justice, are also sacrificed to the spectacle of group survival. Rationality is never used for the refinement of sensibility, even for the group itself, but for the spectacular consolidation of power at all costs. Ultimately, South African culture, in the hands of whites, the dominant force, is incapable of nurturing a civilisation based on the perfection of the individual in order to permit maximum social creativity. Consequently, we have a society of posturing and sloganeering; one that frowns upon subtlety of thought and feeling, and never permits the sobering power of contemplation, of close analysis, and the mature acceptance of failure, weakness, and limitations. It is totally heroic. Even the progressive side has been domesticated by the hegemony of spectacle. For example, it will lambast interiority in character portrayal as bourgeois subjectivity. The entire ethos permits neither inner dialogue with the self, nor a social public dialogue. It breeds insensitivity, insincerity and delusion. We all know how, at least in the last twenty-five years of our fully conscious life, South Africa was always going to be free in the next five years: a prediction that is the very essence of the culture of spectacle. The powerful, on the other hand have been convinced that they will rule forever. Clearly, the culture of the spectacular, in not permitting itself the growth of complexity, has run its course.

I now want to introduce some of the new work that seems to me to break with this tradition of spectacle. It is as if these writers have said: the spectacular ethos has been well documented and is indelibly a deep aspect of our literary and national history. There should be no anxiety that its legitimate political springs are about to run dry. The water will continue to flow, only it is destined to become sweeter, if only because more life-sustaining minerals, the minute essences, will have been added to it. The three stories to be used as examples of this new trend significantly emerge out of the tense and bitter aftermath of the mass uprising and mass killings of June 16, 1976, another spectacle among spectacles. I want to look at 'The Conversion' by Michael Siluma,[11] 'Man Against Himself' by Joël Matlou,[12] and 'Mamlambo' by Bheki Maseko.[13]

Siluma, to begin with, consciously participates in the spectacle tradition as he opens his story:

> A heavily bandaged head; a puffed-up shiny black face with swollen black eyes reduced to mere slits; a mouth with swollen and broken front teeth. This was the picture in Mxolisi's mind when he entered the bedroom, trying to imagine what his cousin John looked like after what had reportedly befallen him three days before.

There are several other conventional symbols of oppression: John has lost his pass and since he is Xhosa speaking, he is referred to his Bantustan in order to fix his papers. But more immediately, John, a Bachelor of Science graduate working as a computer programmer for an American company, has been short changed by an unscrupulous 'Portuguese or Greek' café owner patronised at lunch time by 'labourers from a nearby construction site'. When John demands his correct change he is urged on by the workers to fight for his rights. He does so, and is severely beaten up by the café owner. A clear case of injustice drawn with all the customary details! The disillusioned figure of an educated African in South African fiction has long become a trope for the illustration of injustice. But there, Siluma parts with tradition.

As John recounts to his visiting cousin, Mxolisi, what took place, we note the tone of self-pity in him. He refers to what happens to him as 'strange things'. But Mxolisi is impatient with this self-pity. There is nothing 'strange' really about what happened to John. It is the experience of African people all the time in South Africa. Bitter with remorse and self-pity, John wants to avenge himself:

> 'You know, I feel like going back to that bloody white man's café and smashing all the windows. Then he could do his damndest,' John thundered, for a moment forgetting the pain in his body.

Traditionally this would be the moment for cheering him for he will have fulfilled the demands of spectacular justice. But as the following passage illustrates, Mxolisi is not impressed:

> 'You argue like a child, John. Look man. There are thousands and thousands of white people with mentalities like that café owner's. Smashing his windows might, according to you, serve the purpose of teaching him a lesson. But others like him might still do the same thing he did to you, perhaps even killing you this time. Apart from satisfying your desire for revenge I still insist that your smashing his windows cannot solve the problem.'

The problem, Mxolisi argues, can only be solved by the unity of the 'discriminated against' through organised struggle. John must join the struggle:

> 'Unity, my cousin. Only when we are united as people who are discriminated against can we manage to solve the problem. We must never think that because we are B.Sc. or B.A. graduates and can earn lots of money that we are immune from the sufferings other black people are forced to endure. We must remember that it is only a matter of WHEN we shall come face to face with these problems, just as you have now.
> 'Only a few months ago I invited you to a Hero's Day commemoration service and you told me you were not a

politician. I hope what has happened to you knocks some commonsense into your so-called educated head.'

We notice immediately that Siluma has moved away from merely reflecting the situation of oppression, from merely documenting it, to offering methods for its redemptive transformation. His story combats, among other things, the tendency to resort to self-pity by the powerless when their situation seems hopeless. His approach is dispassionately analytical. He de-romanticises the spectacular notion of struggle by adopting an analytical approach to the reality before him.

For example, the system is seen to use words to validate false-hood: 'The people at the office of Plural Relations, formerly Bantu Affairs Commissioner, formerly Native Affairs Commissioner . . .' The same institution is given the false impression of having changed by the mere changing of its name. We have an example here of the manipulation of reality with language. The effect of this realisation is also to reveal that *rationality can be detected behind the brutality of the system.*

Previously, it was easy and falsely comforting to portray the enemy as being irrational.[14] Also, John's self-delusion is shattered. Just because he has a good job at an American company, he thinks he has made it, and is free from the problems of his own people. In reality, he has been bought, and turned into a false symbol of legitimation. Thirdly, we learn that knowledge of the existence of oppression does not necessarily enable one to fight it. For example, the fellow Africans at the café, having urged John to fight on, do not help him when he is being severely beaten up in their presence by the café owner. People, without being actually organised, will not necessarily go out to fight for their rights.

The story then, can be seen to work at various levels of analysis.

Siluma has gone beyond spectacle in order to reveal the necessary knowledge of actual reality so that we can purposefully deal with it. The manner in which the story is told reflects its own intentions. The analytical ability of Mxolisi is reflected in the manner in which the story is told so that the story itself is a demonstration of its own intentions. It is an analytical story; a story designed to deliberately break down the barriers of the obvious in order to reveal new possibilities of understanding and action. In other words, Siluma has *rediscovered the ordinary*. In this case, the ordinary is defined as the opposite of the spectacular. The ordinary is sobering rationality; it is the forcing of attention on necessary detail. Paying attention to the ordinary and its methods will result in a significant growth of consciousness. Mongane Serote typifies this attitude in the following words:

> child
> if you stop weeping, you may see
> because that is how knowledge begins.[15]

Where before the South African reality was a symbol of spectacular moral wrong, it is now a direct object of change.

'Man Against Himself' by Joël Matlou forces onto us a terrible problem. If there is a sense of the ordinary that is the very antithesis of spectacle, it is to be found in this story. It displays a sense of the ordinary that may be frustrating and even exasperating. This is a kind of initiation story in which a young man in search of work, is advised to go and look for work at a mine, and there, he grows suddenly into a man. His journey to the mine is a long odyssey of suffering. When he gets to the mine, he undergoes further suffering and humiliation. The terrible working conditions at the mine are amply revealed. The problem we have to deal with in this story is how a man who has undergone such brazen and humiliating exploitation should emerge from the entire experience feeling triumphant.

When he receives his pay, he remarks: 'The money was ninety-six rands. It was for my own work. I risked my life and reason for it.' And as he is leaving the mine, returning home, his money in his pockets, he thinks:

I just thrust it (the money) into my empty pocket and walked out of the main gate towards the bush to free myself. That time life was not endless but everlasting. The earth was once supposed to be flat. Well, so it is, from Hlatini to Northam. That fact does not prevent science from proving that the earth as a whole is spherical. We are still at the stage that life is flat – the distance from birth to death. Yet the probability is that life, too, is spherical and much more extensive and capacious than the hemisphere we know.

Here is deeply philosophical contemplation. Here is the discovery of complexity in a seemingly ordinary and faceless worker. For this faceless worker, life is complex. There is a lot more to it than the inherent simplifications of spectacle. Even under oppression, there are certain fundamental lessons:

> Suffering taught me many things . . . Suffering takes a man from known places to unknown places. Without suffering you are not a man. You will never suffer a second time because you have learned to suffer.

And what powerful writing Matlou can unleash! Listen to him when he sees beautiful girls on his return home:

> When I saw the beautiful girls I thought of my own beautiful sweetheart, my bird of Africa, sea water, razor: green-coloured eyes like a snake, high wooden shoes like a cripple; with soft and beautiful skin, smelling of powder under her armpits like a small child, with black boots for winter like a soldier, and a beautiful figure like she does not eat, sleep, speak or become hungry. And she looks like an artificial girl or electric girl. But she was born of her parents, as I was.

A reader schooled in the tradition of spectacle may very well ask himself anxious questions: is the narrator a man labouring under a form of 'false consciousness'? Is this a man who has succumbed to the pressures of oppression and agreed to become a willing agent of the system? It is easy to disregard this story if the answer to these questions is 'yes'. Yet, would it be wise to do so? Can we easily dismiss the honesty, the piling up of detail, those brilliant flashes of philosophical revelation? Why is it that this man is not our proverbial miner (perhaps a figment of our bourgeois imagination?) who is supposed to present the image of a helpless, exploited victim? How do we account for this apparent ambiguity?

The Oral History Project at the National University of Lesotho has conducted numerous interviews with migrant workers, and has come up with a preliminary study of the group of Basotho who called themselves Russians. One particularly interesting informant named Rantoa declared:

> I did not study. I just see blackness on these things, I can leave my letter at the post office not knowing that it is mine because I did not study. What I have is a natural sense that God gave me – and gifts – as for them they are many.[16]

His has been a life of jail, escape, fights, securing lawyers for the best defense, and a variety of jobs. Rantoa, comment the authors, 'is a man who has consciously developed a philosophy, a set of ideas, drawn from his own experience and which integrates his life and his understandings of it . . . His philosophy is not an abstract one, but emerges from concrete situations. He sees life as a struggle, a fight, in which one must always be consolidating one's forces, undermining the opposition, and developing a strategy which avoids the obvious, frontal attack and strikes where it is not expected'. The remarkable convergence and similarity of philosophy between Matlou's character and this real life informant is too striking to be ignored.

The school of criticism which favours explicit political themes will be exasperated by the seeming lack of direct political consciousness on the part of Matlou's character. But we must contend with the fact that even under the most oppressive of conditions, people are always trying and struggling to maintain a semblance of normal social order. They will attempt to apply tradition and custom to manage their day to day family problems: they will resort to socially acquired behaviour patterns to eke out a means of subsistence. They apply systems of values that they know. Often those values will undergo changes under certain pressing conditions. The transformation of those values constitutes the essential drama in the lives of ordinary people.

The range of problems is ordinary enough but constitutes the active social consciousness of most people: will I like my daughter's boyfriends or prospective husband? how do I deal with my attraction to my friend's wife? what will my child become? Relatives can be a nuisance; someone I despise has bought a better car than mine; the principal is messing up the school, I'm going to try to be the next principal. The list is endless. We are confronted here with the honesty of the self in confrontation with itself. Literature cannot give us lessons, but it can only provide a very compelling context to examine an infinite number of ethical issues which have a bearing on the sensitisation of people towards the development of the entire range of culture.

So how do we deal with Matlou's character. The experience of working in the mines has a human dimension to it seldom accepted; a personal testimony that shatters the liberal image of pathetic sufferers. We are faced with the validity of his experience against the problematic nature of the method of presenting experience. This is the kind of tension that is the very substance of narrative complexity. That the writer did not explore the ultimate implications of his materials is no doubt connected to his inexperience both as a writer and in the inadequacy of his education. But the significance of the story is that the writer has given us an honest rendering of the subjective experience of his character. There is no unearned heroism here; instead there is the unproclaimed heroism of the ordinary person.

Finally, the crux of the matter is that it is natural for us to want to condemn the obvious exploitative conditions of work in the mines. But we should be careful that condemnation does not extend to condemning the necessity for work and the satisfaction that can result from it. Indeed, that aspect of Matlou's story which celebrates the values of work and experience should be rescued and separated from the conditions of exploitation in which that work is done. The necessary political vilification of exploitation should be separated from the human triumph associated with work, a triumph which constitutes a positive value for the future. Matlou confronts us with the painful dialectic of suffering and the sense of redemption that can result from it.

We shall spend less space on the next story because I think the point has been made already. 'Mamlambo' is a story that participates in that aspect of the folk tradition that concerns luck. How does one come across the luck to push one towards success and the achievement of goals? One can turn to an *inyanga*, or *isangoma*, to a faith healer or to other similar people who are believed to have control over the forces of nature. In this case, a woman, living in the backyards of posh white suburbs in Johannesburg, has had no luck getting a regular partner. She turns to an *inyanga* who seems to live somewhere in the city too. The *inyanga* gives the woman Umamlambo, the mythical snake that brings luck to anyone who possesses it. Indeed, the woman gets a Malawian lover who marries her. But she has to pass on the snake. This she does in a most amusing manner. As the story ends, she sees below her, Johannesburg getting smaller and smaller as the plane takes to the sky with her on her way to Malawi.

Of the three stories, this is probably the most thematically ordinary. A woman simply wants to get a man. She desires the security of a lover, a husband. Yet what vibrancy of imagination is displayed by the writer! African folk culture has an independent life of its own right bang in the middle of 'civilisation', of western 'rationality'. The surrounding 'superior' civilisation is rendered of no consequence whatsoever. It is as good as not there. The experience is accorded a validity that does not have to justify itself at all. Bheki Maseko's stories always remind me of Haitian paintings: vibrant with colour, a combination of naturalistic and fantastic elements. Indeed, as Soyinka asserts,[17] the rational and non-rational constitute a single sphere of reality in African lore. Bheki Maseko's stories represent this living continuity between the past and the present. What we have here is a story of escape and fulfilment, but it is the imaginative cultural context evoked that, in the final analysis, is most memorable.

It now remains for us to draw some theoretical conclusions from the phenomenon before us. It should be stated from the onset that the overwhelming injustice inherent in the South African social formation is something that cannot be ignored under any circumstances. For this reason, it is natural to expect that people engaged in every human endeavour ought to make a contribution towards the eradication of injustice. The problem, as we have seen, is that it now appears as if the means of combating the situation have become too narrow and constricting. This weakness has been premised on the demand that everything must make a spectacular political statement. According to this attitude, Maseko's and Matlou's stories could very easily be dismissed as irrelevant since they offer no obvious political insight. Even if Siluma's story could qualify, its message though, could easily be embraced at the expense of the sobering details such as given above. The habit of looking at the spectacle has forced us to gloss over the nooks and crannies.

The significance of these stories for me is that they point the way in which South African literature might possibly develop. By rediscovering the ordinary, the stories remind us necessarily, that the problems of the South African social formation are complex and all embracing; that they cannot be reduced to a single, simple formulation. In fact, one novel has already attempted an infusion of the ordinary into the spectacle. Serote's *To Every Birth Its Blood*[18] attempts to deal with the ordinary concerns of people while placing those problems within the broad political situation in the country. In the end, though, the spectacle takes over and the novel throws away the vitality of the tension generated by the dialectic between the personal and public.

These three stories remind us that the ordinary daily lives of people should be the direct focus of political interest because they constitute the *very content* of the struggle, for the struggle involves people not abstractions. If it is a new society we seek to bring about in South Africa then that newness will be based on a direct concern with the way people actually live. That means a range of complex ethical issues involving man-man, man-woman, woman-woman, man-nature, man-society relationships. These kinds of concerns are destined to find their way into our literature, making it more complex and richer. As the struggle intensifies, for example, there will be accidental deaths, missing children, loss of property, disruption of the general social fabric resulting in tremendous inconvenience. Every individual will be forced, in a most personal manner, to take a position with regard to the entire situation. The majority will be riddled with doubts. Yet, there will be those marked by fate to experience the tragedy of carrying the certitudes to the level of seeming fanaticism. It will be the task of literature to provide an occasion within which vistas of inner capacity are opened up. The revolution, as Lenin pointed out, will not necessarily take place out of every 'revolutionary situation'. Also essential is the subjective 'capacity of the revolutionary *class* to take the mass revolutionary actions that are strong enough to smash (or break up) the old government, which, not even in time of crises, will "fall" unless it is "dropped" '.[19] The new literature can contribute to the development of this subjective capacity of the people to be committed, but only on the basis of as complete a knowledge of themselves and the objective situation as possible. The growth of consciousness is a necessary ingredient of this subjective capacity.

It is germane at this point to point out that there are some serious weaknesses in the three stories discussed above. In 'Mamlambo' for example, the flight to Malawi does not really go together with the growth of consciousness on the part of the protagonist on the very question of matrimony, on the question of luck, on the question of leaving to start a new life in Malawi. Matlou's character also, sees no social implications of his triumph beyond himself. Some of these literary deficiencies can be attributed to the intellectually stunting effects of apartheid and Bantu education. These writers have however made superhuman efforts to explore life beyond the narrow focus of an oppressive education.

The more serious problem, because it is self-inflicted, is the fact that the intellectual tradition governing either politics or literature has not broadened the scope of its social interest. Political visions of the future have not reached art with sufficient, let alone committed, theoretical clarity.

Perhaps it was this realisation that prompted Soyinka to observe that South African writers might yet be envied for their invidious position by their brothers up north.[20] Young writers appear to have taken up the challenge, albeit unwittingly. They seemed prepared to confront the human tragedy together with the immense challenging responsibility to create a new society. This demands an uncompromisingly toughminded creative will to build a new civilisation. And no civilisation worth the name will emerge without the payment of disciplined and rigorous attention to detail.

NOTES

1. Roland Barthes, *Mythologies*, Annette Lavers (trans.), (London: Jonathan Cape, 1972), pp.15–25.
2. Roland Barthes, p.15.
3. T.T. Moyana, 'Problems of a Creative Writer in South Africa', in *Aspects of South African Literature*, C. Heywood (ed.), (London: Heinemann, 1976), pp.95–6.
4. Roland Barthes, p.18.
5. See *English in Africa*, March 1975, Vol.12, No.1.
6. Alex La Guma 'Coffee for the Road', in *Modern African Stories*, Ellis Ayitey Komey and Ezekiel Mphahlele (eds.), (London: Faber and Faber, 1964), pp.85–94.
7. Dennis Brutus, *A Simple Lust*, (London: Heinemann AWS, 1973), p.19.
8. See, for example, Mbulelo Mzamane, 'Politics and Literature in Africa: A Review', *Staffrider*, Vol.3, No.4, December/January 1980, pp.43–5.
9. Chinweizu et al. *Towards the Decolonisation of African Literature*, Vol.I, (Nigeria: Fourth Dimension, 1980).
10. Roland Barthes, p.19.

11. *Staffrider*, Vol.2, No.4, November/December 1979, pp.6–8.

12. *Staffrider*, Vol.2, No.4, November/December 1979, pp.24–8.

13. *Staffrider*, Vol.5, No.1, 1982, pp.22–7.

14. See, for example, Heribert Adam, *Modernising Racial Domination*, (Los Angeles: University of California Press, 1971).

15. Mongane Serote, *Tsetlo*, (Johannesburg: Ad. Donker, 1974), p.10.

16. Jeff Guy and Motlatsi Thabane, 'The Ma-Rashea: A Participant's Perspective', in *Class, Community and Conflict*, Belinda Bozzoli (ed.), (Ravan Press, Johannesburg 1987), p.441.

17. Wole Soyinka, *Myth, Literature and the African World*, (Cambridge: C.U.P., 1978), p.65.

18. Mongane Serote, *To Every Birth Its Blood*, (Johannesburg: Ravan Press, 1981).

19. Lenin, 'The Symptoms of a Revolutionary Situation', in *The Lenin Anthology*, Robert C. Tucker (ed.), (New York: Norton, 1975), p.276.

20. Wole Soyinka, 'The Writer in a Modern African State', in *The Writer in Modern Africa*, Per Wastberg (ed.), (Uppsala: Scandinavian Institute of African Studies, 1968), p.15.

3

❖ ❖ ❖

REDEFINING RELEVANCE

Recently, I have suggested that what has been called protest literature may have run its course in South Africa.[1] It is my intention here to probe further into this evaluation by attempting to bring out clearly its theoretical foundations. Basically, the problem is that 'protest literature' appears to have lost its objective basis. The fact that much of the writing produced in the townships of South Africa since 1976 still reproduced this protest tradition, with little modification, reveals what seems to me to be the characteristics of a socially entrenched manner of thinking about the South African reality; a manner of thinking which, over the years, has gathered its own momentum and now reproduces itself uncritically. It is like a train the driver of which has lost control, and it runs dangerously on its fixed rails, passing, with great speed, even where it is supposed to stop. The difference might be that in the case of the train, its driver will know almost immediately that he or she is in trouble. He is, after all, not the train. In the case of the writer of 'protest literature', on the other hand, it may not be so easy for him or her to separate himself momentarily from his mind.

The problem is to be located in the nature of South African oppression and how its unabating pervasiveness has induced, almost universally in the country, a distinctive manner of thinking about the socio-political realities, an epistemology in which reality is conceived purely in terms of a total polarity of absolutes. Such an epistemology is, of course, entirely understandable: South African society *is* a highly polarised society. It is understandable that its constituent polarities should dominate the thinking of its citizens. This outcome is even more predictable when we realise that one major characteristic of South African society is that the racist rulers have done very little to hide the polarities produced by their terrible form of domination. On the contrary, these polarities have been and continue to be displayed fully. There can be no doubt, for example, about who is in power and who is not; no doubt about who commands vast resources of wealth, and who lives in abject poverty. Nor is there any doubt, in general terms, why things are the way they are.

In general, this situation has resulted in two distinct perceptions of their reality by South Africans. For the oppressed, political knowledge came to be equated with the recognition of the blatant injustice which occurs in various forms throughout the country. To know has been to know how badly one has been treated. Every other thing is irrelevant unless it is perceived as contributing to the extension of this knowledge. Beyond that, having this knowledge implied that one either gave in to the bleak reality revealed, or committed oneself to removing this general condition of injustice. How this was to be actually carried out would depend on the means that are available to the oppressed at any particular moment.

On the other hand, for the ruling white racists, knowledge has been equated with the quest for mastery over the political and economic means of maintaining privilege and domination. To know has been to find ways of maintaining dominance. As a result, the white racists have, over the years, built a complex structure of government and an array of other social and economic institutions, all of which have diversified the sources and the means of acquiring information and knowledge for the preservation of political and economic domination.

In order for us to get a practical sense of this situation, it may be useful to examine a recent drama between African miners and the white mine managers of the Impala Platinum Mine, in that part of

South Africa called Bophuthatswana. This particular drama can be viewed as a telling analogy of the history of the African struggle for freedom in South Africa.

Recently in South Africa some 23 000 African miners were summarily dismissed from their jobs. This figure is so immense that it is by itself a measure of how spectacular the play of South African oppression can be. The figure, however, is small when we consider the fact that the dismissed men came from families who depended on them for a livelihood. So there is a real sense in which it was not just the miners who were dismissed, but also at least 100 000 other people. But the drama of South African oppression is such that it has become customary for its observers, both those involved and those on the sidelines, to focus on its most observable aberrations. We concentrate on the 23 000 men, the most observable proof of injustice, and consequently, the most immediate in terms of the imperatives of political activism. The other hundred thousand maintain a blurred presence, seldom becoming a serious factor of analysis and reflection. They were not there at the scene of the action. This point I shall come back to later.

The two parties involved in this labour dispute reveal their perceptions of the problems before them in the following manner. Following their dismissal, a representative of the striking miners observed: 'Management does not have sympathy for people. They don't listen to what we have to say. They regard us as animals. That is why it is possible for them to do this.'[2] On the other hand, a representative of the mine management observed: 'you run into a point where they get completely unreasonable. The alternative is to get rid of the whole labour force and replace them. There is a condition of massive unemployment in the country and that encourages us to take this kind of action.'[3]

Firstly, at the most immediate pre-critical level, we cannot fail to recognise the 'them-us' polarity. There is no need even to state that the management is white and the miners are black. The 'them-us' polarity already exists within that other larger polarity. Secondly, the miners seem to be almost completely powerless against the massive power of the management. The management controls the entire means of livelihood; it controls a complex organisation which is itself firmly placed within the even more complex structure of exploitation characteristic of South African society. Furthermore, the habit of working within a complex system develops the manipulative capacity of those in control of the system to take advantage of the laws of that system for their own exclusive benefit.

Against all this, the miners, having been effectively denied the opportunity to create comparable adversary systems of their own, have had no opportunity to develop their own manipulative capacity.[4] They have nothing of comparable organisational status to set in motion in order to defend and project their interests. Indeed, all they have is their voice, and the capacity of that voice, under the circumstances, is limited largely to articulating grievance. It draws its strength and validity from the moral law: 'Management does not have sympathy for people.' But, as this instance shows, the moral law can be tragically impotent in the face of economic laws that do not recognise its intrinsic validity.

It seems clear that in this situation the structural position of the miners (the 'aggrieved') permits them, in response to their terrible ordeal, very few options besides the mere articulation of grievance. The structural position of the miners in this case, is identical, it seems to me, to the structural position of the oppressed majority in South Africa during the time in the country's history when protest literature flourished: the period between 1948 and 1961. It was a period characterised by a greater institutionalisation of repression. There was much organised resistance, but it was often brutally crushed. This increased repression created a charged atmosphere in which the resulting articulation of grievance, at both organisational and personal levels, became most ironically the very index of powerlessness.

The result of this situation was that, increasingly, the material dimensions of oppression soon assumed a rhetorical form in which the three chief rhetorical aspects were: one, the identification and highlighting of instances of general oppression; two, the drawing of appropriate moral conclusions from the revealed evidence and, three, the implicit belief in the inherent persuasiveness of the moral position. The identified outward evidence of oppression then, prompted a rhetoric which emphasised the moral embitterment of the oppressed. The rhetoric began to dominate the consciousness of the oppressed in such a way that they could easily lose the sense of the actual mechanisms of their own oppression. In other words, the rhetoric of protest began to replace the necessary commitment to engaging the forces of oppression through paying critical attention to the concrete social and political details of that oppression. This kind of replacement can have devastating effects on the capacity of the oppressed to develop a creatively analytical approach to their predicament.

For example, the pervasive images of wealth and poverty, of power and powerlessness, of knowledge and ignorance, of form and formlessness, may easily lead to the simplification and trivial-isation of moral perception. The oppressed need only cast their eyes around to see a universal confirmation of their status. Evil abounds. There is no need for further analysis. The mere pointing of a finger provides proof. In this situation, the rhetorical identification of social and political evil may easily become coincident with political and intellectual insight. In reality, the recognition of a source of grievance does not necessarily imply that one understands a possible range of political implications which that recognition may entail. This problem, as has been hinted above, might give us some understanding of the effect of oppression on the general intellectual development of the oppressed.

It needs to be stated that the moral position, when we consider the overall circumstances in which recourse to it was taken, was, of course, entirely valid and correct. What one is attempting to do here is hint at its possible limitations. This task is essential when a particular way of viewing reality gathers its own momentum over a period of time and becomes a predominant mode of perception even when the conditions justifying its existence have passed. At that point the mode of perception, by failing to transcend its own lim-itations, can become part of the oppression it sought to understand

and undermine. It does not do so intentionally, of course: it simply becomes trapped. Such entrapment may even lead to the development of a dangerous predisposition to reform rather than to radical change.

Indeed, the entrapment of resistance in an unreflective rhetoric of protest could easily be one of the sources of reactionary politics even among the oppressed. Where the dialectic between good and evil has been simplified, the predisposition, on the part of the powerful, to satisfy the moral sense of the oppressed with minimum concessions asserts itself. This happens at those moments when the oppressors feel that it is in their own interests to make concessions. Such concessions, if they can be perceived as significant gains, particularly by the oppressed, can lead to the politics of reform. Reform easily appeals to the moral sentiment; whereas radical change relies on continuous critical engagement with reality. Not only is nothing taken for granted, in addition, the reformist manipulations of the oppressor can be anticipated and neutralised. That the oppressed can easily fail to recognise the manipulative intent of their oppressors can be attributed to the fact that an uncritical rhetoric of protest can easily impair the capacity of the oppressed to think strategically. Easily believing an abstract moral code, they become victims of false hopes. However, that the moral sentiment can be severely compromised, does not invalidate it; it is simply that the conditions in which it can continue to inspire confidence ought to be brought into being.

I have so far devoted much of this paper to a discussion of the general situation in order to suggest the unenviably onerous position of the writer in it: to indicate how writers can themselves be encapsulated by the material and intellectual culture of oppression, and how difficult it can be for them to achieve a transcendence. For example, the writers of the fifties and sixties, being part of the political climate that they wrote about, codified the predominant modes of political perception by transforming those perceptions into literary figures. This led to the predominance of certain themes, characters, and situations which were welded into a recognisable grammar of what came to be called 'protest literature'.

We were shown in this literature the predictable drama between ruthless oppressors and their pitiful victims; ruthless policemen and their cowed, bewildered prisoners; brutal farmers and their exploited farm hands; cruel administrative officials in a horribly impersonal bureaucracy, and the bewildered residents of the township, victims of that bureaucracy; crowded trains and the terrible violence that goes on in them among the oppressed; and a variety of similar situations. Of course, what we are looking at here is a trend. There were other writings that handled the issues very differently.

For the bulk of the writings, however, the grammar of protest inherent in them is, as has been suggested above, entirely understandable when we consider not only the structural position of the oppressed African population as a whole, but also the social position of the writers within the oppressed population. Many of them were either teachers or journalists or both, more often than not with a protestant (usually Anglican) educational and/or religious background. It is understandable that they should express the predicament of the oppressed not in terms of what structurally produced it, but in terms of its implied opposite: white political and economic power and privilege. There, lay the moral problem. The writing sharpened the moral sense which, under the circumstances, may have been the only effective way by which to validate and maintain the sense of legitimate political opposition. From this perspective, moral opposition should properly be regarded as both historically and politically apt.

If protest writing in the fifties was in tune with protest politics, protest writing in the sixties and seventies was not entirely in tune with political developments. Protest politics *effectively* ends in 1968 with the establishment of the South African Students Organisation (SASO), and the Black Consciousness Movement (BCM).[5] But protest writing, significantly, did not end with the end of protest politics. It simply assumed a different form of protest. Certainly, it reflected the militancy and confrontational attitude of the new movement, but while the new movement represented a decisively new political orientation, the writing that it inspired represented no remarkable contribution to literary figuration. The new writing did not appropriate the new analytical sophistication of the BCM into its own handling of literary form.

The reason for this situation is not hard to recognise. The political analysis of the role of literature in the struggle for liberation did not go beyond the general agreement that literature must be committed. A rhetorical attitude toward literature was adapted which did not analytically spell out how literature could express its commitment. What we have, as a result, is protest literature that merely changed emphasis: from the moral evil of apartheid, to the existential and moral worth of blackness; from moral indignation, to anger; from relatively self-composed reasonableness, to uncompromising bitterness; from the exterior manifestation of oppression, to the interior psychology of that oppression. That may be why the bulk of the writing was poetry. But while the poetry turns its attention towards the self, it is still very conscious of the white 'other' Although the new writing has begun to make a move away from that preoccupation with the 'other', it is still rooted in the emotional and intellectual polarities of South African oppression as discussed above. And that is the point at which protest literature turns into a pathology: when objective conditions no longer justify or support an entirely emotional or moral attitude.

There is much to indicate that the structural position of the oppressed in South Africa has altered significantly, particularly from the time of the labour strikes that shook the country from 1973 onwards.[6] The phenomenal growth of the economy up to that time is clearly responsible for a significant change in relations of power between the oppressed and the oppressor. Increased industrialisation had enhanced the capacity of the working people to assert their collective power. The intensity of the labour disputes, for example, led eventually to the capitulation of the state to demands for the legal unionisation of labour. Meanwhile, the events of June 1976 also helped to consolidate the new relations of power. Clearly, the structural position of the oppressed now was such that they could no longer be cowed into a submission reminiscent of the fifties. The inevitable growth and consolidation of this new power would definitely lead to new general perceptions of what was possible. While previously the range of what was possible had been severely limited by the condition of powerlessness, now the newly found power could extend that range considerably in all kinds of directions. Suddenly, the possibilities became immense.

The rest of this essay is premised on the belief that the greatest challenge of the South African revolution is in the search for ways of thinking, ways of perception, that will help to break down the closed epistemological structures of South African oppression. Structures which can severely compromise resistance by dominating thinking itself. The challenge is to free the entire social imagination of the oppressed from the laws of perception that have characterised apartheid society. For writers this means freeing the creative process itself from those very laws. It means extending the writer's perception of what can be written about, and the means and methods of writing.

It seems to me that a redemptive approach can begin to be formulated when South African writers ask the question: where is the struggle in South Africa at the moment? Many recent events in the country have led inevitably to that question. For example, the prolonged school boycott that began in 1976, and still continues today, has finally led to similar questions with regard to education: where do we go from here? What kind of education do we want for the future? Beyond that, questions have been asked in relation to other aspects of society: what legal system do we envisage for a new South Africa? What system of public health will adequately cater for the health needs of all citizens? What kind of cultural policy are we going to evolve? What are we going to do with ethnicity? All these questions and more, have been prompted by the momentum of current events in which the state has been found to be increasingly unable to manage society without recourse to more repressive measures even as it speaks of reform: a situation that reflects a near total bankruptcy of vision on the part of the ruling Nationalist Party.

Significantly, the act of asking such questions already suggests that the closed structures of thought under the culture of apartheid oppression are cracking. A vast new world is opening up, for the possible answers to the questions are as infinite as the immensity of the questions themselves.

It seems to me that these are the most important questions that have ever been asked by our people in recent times, and they are questions that can only be answered fully from as complete an understanding as possible of the position from which they have been asked. For example, as far as education is concerned, the oppressed have reached a position at which an aspect of the structure of domination has, through their own actions, been rendered largely inoperative. The question is: what next? A point has been reached, therefore, at which the oppressed have to ask themselves some fundamental questions about the future of education and its contribution towards a new and free society. What is at issue now is no longer the moral condemnation of Bantu Education; rather, it is the creation of a new kind of education. This change in understanding is reflected in the fact that initially, the political act of challenging the legitimacy of education under apartheid was carried out under the slogan of 'liberation first, education later'. However, following further reflection on developments, this slogan was rejected. It was replaced by one which recognised the need for education even during the process of struggle: 'people's education for people's power'.

The overall significance of these questions is that they indicate the beginning of the freeing of the oppressed social imagination from the constraints of attempting to envision the future under the limitations of oppression. The future, at this point, is perceived as being possible only with the contribution of the oppressed themselves as decision makers. That attitude of the oppressed brings with it heavy responsibilities for them. It suggests the appearance of challenging yet daunting tasks, amenable to no easy solutions, for in it are springs of a new society. One of the central tasks of an alternative ideology, in this situation, is to provide, among other things, new ways of thinking about the future of the country.

The starting point is the need and demand of the oppressed for liberation. The political imperatives of that demand are the positing of an alternative future followed by the seizure of state power. For the political activist, the task seems clear. For the producer of cultural artefacts, on the other hand, the situation may not be so clear because his role as well as that of his work, has not been as clearly defined. The South African writer, in particular, has not begun to ask some fundamental questions about his role, as well as that of his artistic practice. By and large, he appears to have handed over this task to the political activist, who may not himself have articulated a comprehensively analytical position on the role of the arts in the struggle. This situation, it seems to me, has been responsible for the rather slow growth of South African literature.

The problem has been that questions about art and society have been easily settled after a general consensus about commitment. This has led to the prescription of solutions even before all the problems have been discovered and analysed. The writer, as a result, has tended to plunge into the task of writing without fully grappling with the theoretical demands of that task in all its dimensions. Armed with notions of artistic commitment still constrained by outmoded protest-bound perceptions of the role of art and of what constitutes political relevance in art, he set about reproducing a dead-end. Consequently, the limited range of explorable experience characteristic of writing under the protest ethos has continued to plague much of South African writing. We can perhaps begin to edge away from that situation by addressing the issue of the nature of art as well as the question of what constitutes relevance under a situation of radical flux such as obtains in South Africa today.

One accusation that has often been levelled at writers, particularly in those countries hungry for radical change, is that many of them have not offered solutions to the problems they may have graphically revealed. It seems to me that this accusation has been based on a set of premises by which the nature of the relationship between art and society could never be adequately disclosed. More often than not, the accusation has been premised on the demand that artists produce works that will incite people to political action, something which, most people will agree, is strictly speaking the task of the professional propagandist. The propagandist generally aims at immediate action. His intentions are entirely practical.

The artist, on the other hand, although desiring action, often with as much passion as the propagandist, can never be entirely free from the rules of irony. Irony is the literary manifestation of the principle of contradiction. Its fundamental law, for the literary arts in particular, is that everything involving human society is in a constant state of flux; that the dialectic between appearance and reality in the conduct of human affairs is always operative and constantly problematic, and that consequently, in the representation of human reality, nothing can be taken for granted. If the writer has an ideological goal, and he always has, he has to reach that goal through a serious and inevitable confrontation with irony, and must earn his conclusions through the resulting sweat. And when he has won that battle, he will most likely leave us, the readers, more committed, but only on the necessary condition that we have been made to reflect deeply on the nature and implications of our commitment in the context of the compelling human drama presented before us.

The relationship between politics and art is by definition always mediated by reflection. With this understanding, we distinguish only between immediate action, on the one hand, and delayed action, on the other. But this distinction does not necessarily enable us to make a mechanical choice between politics and art: rather, it enables us to participate in the dialectic between the two. To understand this is to understand the creative possibilities of both.

The way seems clear now for us to deal with the question of 'relevance'. The more limited understanding of the relationship between politics and art would define as relevant any subject or act that is perceived to contribute dramatically to the struggle for liberation. The operative word here is 'dramatic'. What is dramatic is often defined according to the imperatives of *real politik*. According to this definition, the dramatic can easily be determined: strike action, demonstrations; alternatively, the brutality of the oppressive system in a variety of ways.

It should not be difficult to realise that from the point of view of the South African writer today, the range of what is traditionally regarded as relevant is tragically limited in comparison to the complex structure of the oppression itself. The system does not only send tanks into the townships. It does a lot more as its strategies for domination have diversified to take advantage of a complex industrial society. It works at subtle co-optation; it tries to produce a middle class; it sets off a series of diplomatic initiatives, overt and covert; it seeks to create normalcy by insidiously spreading a hegemony that the oppressed are designed to absorb without being conscious of actually doing so through film, radio, television and a range of publications. It may even permit a controlled 'experimental' opening up of white private schools to African children where the latter can absorb a wide range of largely liberal hegemonic practices that may ultimately not be in their own interests. Central to all these sophisticated strategies of containment is the rampant growth and promotion of consumerism ranging from fashion through cars right up to houses. In other words, the system mobilises its own range of extra-governmental institutions in an attempt to impose and propagate its hegemony. In this sense, it responds as a total system.

Clearly, if it is the entire society that has to be recreated, then no aspect of that society can be deemed irrelevant to the progress of liberation. Clearly, the broader the focus, the more inclusive, then the more manifold and more complex the attack. In this context, relevance, for the post-protest South African writer, begins, as it should, with the need for the seizure of state power. For the writer, this need also fragments into a concern with an infinite number of specific social details which are the very objects of artistic reflection; and, it is such social details which constitute the primary reason why the struggle occurs in the first place.

Most paradoxically, for the writer, the *immediate* problem, just at the point at which he sits down to write his novel, is not the seizure of power. Far from it. His immediate aim is a radically contemplative state of mind in which the objects of contemplation are that range of social conditions which are the major ingredients of social consciousness. Exclusion of any on the grounds that they do not easily lend themselves to dramatic political statement will limit the possibilities of any literary revolution, by severely limiting the social range on which to exercise its imagination.

What are the practical implications of all this? We have already seen how the structural status of the oppressed within South African society has altered radically. The implications of this newly found power are the writer's starting point. That power is clearly aware of itself, and that self-consciousness is destined to grow. But, judging from the fundamental questions being asked, as shown above, that power is still not fully aware of what it can actually achieve. Details still have to be worked out. And this is where the writer's role becomes crucial. It is his task to contribute effectively to the consolidation of that power, by consolidating consciousness of it at all levels of society. He can do so in a number of ways.

First of all, there must be a freeing of the imagination in which what constitutes the field of relevance is extended considerably. What is relevant is the entire community of the oppressed. For example, politics is not confined only to the seizure of state power; it can also be the decision by members of a township women's burial society to replace a corrupt leader with a new one. The significance of the moral and ethical issues that may be involved in this matter, together with whatever insightful revelations may be made about the interplay of human motives, ought not to be underestimated. They have a direct bearing on the quality of social awareness.

This whole issue is so important that a few more examples are in order. Firstly, for a highly industrialised society such as South Africa, there is a tragic paucity of imaginative recreations of the confrontation between the oppressed and the tools of science. Supposing a character wants to study science: what goes on in his mind when he makes that decision? What is his vision of the social role of the scientific endeavour? Turgenev, for example, in *Fathers and Sons*, provides a compelling view of the impact of the scientific method on human behaviour in the context of nineteenth century Russia. Alternatively, what kind of relationships are created between a worker in a factory and his machine? The answer to this question is not necessarily obvious. Will he necessarily feel oppressed and alienated, as traditional radical wisdom would suggest? There is much to suggest that this confrontation is much more problematic than is often assumed.

Secondly, we have, for better or for worse, a group of politicians in the so-called independent states of South Africa. Stooges, no doubt in the total scheme of things. But what are the intricacies of their flawed diplomatic practice? We have no literature of diplomacy which can reveal the human dimension of this barren politics. The artist should help the reader condemn a stooge while understanding something of his motivations. That way the reader learns something about the psychology of the co-opted. The aesthetics of protest would be content to kill off the man, thus enacting what might be necessary, from the point of view of natural justice but leaving us with no knowledge.

Thirdly, the pressures of modern life on the family have been immense. We know some of the causes: migrant labour, influx control laws, and political exile, for example. Protest literature, commendably, has kept these causes in our minds. But what, really, has happened to the family itself? Currently, a most painful clash of generations has emerged in the townships between parents and children. It appears in the main to result from the perception by the youth that their parents did not do enough to combat their oppression. This situation has momentarily catapulted the youth into the forefront of the liberation struggle with some agonising consequences for the structure of authority not only in the community at large, but also in the family itself. Many values that have governed family relationships have been changed. What happened to those values, and how have new emergent ones helped to bring about either relief or more misery to families and the community?

Fourthly, the energetic and creative world of sport and fashion has seldom been treated beyond the sensationalism of the popular press. Consequently, we have no body of imaginative fiction that explores how popular culture in the hands of the state and big business can compromise severely a revolutionary consciousness. Sport and fashion as subjects of serious fiction have been dismissed too easily as irrelevant to politics. Indeed, since Mphahlele's 'Griek on a Stolen Piano',[7] that particular theme has not received much imaginative attention.

Lastly, I have commented in the past on the lack of compelling imaginative recreations of rural life in our literature.[8] All we know about are dejected peasants, suffering pathetically under a tyrannical Boer farmer. Alternatively, the peasants are the focus of Christian evangelism. Clearly, rural culture as a serious fictional theme needs to be revisited.

Beyond these five examples, the settings as well as the themes that can be imaginatively explored are infinite.

One other way by which the South African writer can move effectively into the post-protest era is by working towards a radical displacement of the white oppressor as an active, dominant player in the imagination of the oppressed. This tactical absence will mean that the writer can consolidate the sense of a viable, psychologically self-sufficient community among the oppressed. This attitude can only work, though, if the writer genuinely believes in the oppressed, in the first instance, as makers of the future. This implies a radical rearrangement of the dialectical poles. Where the thesis was the oppressor, it is now the oppressed confidently introducing new definitions of the future to which the oppressor will have of necessity to respond. The latter, no longer having the intellectual and imaginative capability to initiate redemptive action, has to be relegated to the reactive pole of the dialectic. He is no longer in possession of the initiative.

Finally, there must be an accompanying change of discourse from the rhetoric of oppression to that of process and exploration. This would imply an open-endedness in the use of language, a search for originality of expression and a sensitivity to dialogue. The complexity of the daily problems of living in fact coincides with the demands of the creative act. As the writer begins to work on that story, he may not know where it is headed, and how it is going to work towards its conclusion; but he has to find a way. That means a search for appropriate form and technique, which would enable him to grasp the complexity and render it understandable. Here, the question of technique does not mean a rarefied, formal, and disembodied attempt at innovation for its own sake. On the contrary, technique implies the attempt to find the best possible ways of extending social perception through appropriateness of form. Technique, then, is inseparable from the exploration of human perception.

Earlier, in my discussion of the mine dispute, I made reference to the fact that at least 100 000 people were dismissed by the mine management. It is towards the silent 100 000 that our writers must now turn their attention. I mean this analogically, of course. The operative principle of composition in post-protest literature is that it should probe beyond the observable facts, to reveal new worlds where it was previously thought they did not exist, and to reveal process and movement where they were hidden. This way, the social imagination of the oppressed can be extended considerably and made ready in concrete terms to deal with the demands of a complex future. The aim is to extend the range of personal and social experience as far as possible in order to contribute to bringing about a highly conscious, sensitive new person in a new society. This, it seems to me, is the function of art in, and its contribution to, the ongoing revolution in South Africa.

These observations, it should be stated, are put forward not as laws, but as possible guidelines by which our writers can conduct a debate and bring to bear further analysis on the tasks of writers and the role of their art in the unfolding revolution in South Africa. The tasks themselves are immense and challenging; I believe a vigorous discussion of them will, in itself, be a significant act of freedom.

NOTES

1. See Njabulo S. Ndebele, 'The Rediscovery of the Ordinary: Some New Writings in South Africa', *Journal of Southern African Studies*, Vol.12, No.2, 1986.
2. *Weekly Mail*, Johannesburg, January 10 to 16, 1986.
3. Ibid.
4. Although miners outside of the Bantustans have access to trade union organisations, those working in Bophuthatswana at the time of this incident in 1986 could not legally form unions.
5. Of course, the major liberation movements, ANC and PAC, in opting for the armed struggle immediately following their banning in 1961, had declared the end of the politics of protest. But, at the time, the new approach did not have a lasting impact in the country.
6. See for example, The Institute for Industrial Education, *The Durban Strikes, 1973*: '*Human beings with Souls*', (Durban-Johannesburg: Ravan Press, 1974).
7. Ezekiel Mphahlele, 'Griek on a Stolen Piano', in *In Corner B*, (Nairobi: East African Publishing House, 1967), pp.37–61.
8. Njabulo S. Ndebele, 'Turkish Tales and Some Thoughts on South African Literature', *Staffrider*, Vol.6, No.1, 1984.

4

❖ ❖ ❖

ACTORS AND INTERPRETERS:
POPULAR CULTURE AND PROGRESSIVE
FORMALISM

I must begin by letting you know that when I received the invitation to speak on this occasion, I agonised over the political ethics of coming here. It cannot be pretended that the existence of this institution, together with the political entity in which it exists, is not a problematic issue. I was aware of the aggressiveness with which this institution strove to cultivate for itself an image of the kind of progressive normalcy associated with similar institutions under less contentious circumstances. I was aware, for example, of publications from here, being dutifully sent to other universities in the subcontinent; of vigorous recruitment efforts; of massive building projects; and of other impressively ambitious plans. And I noted the irony that this aggressiveness, given the total historical circumstances in which this institution exists, could legitimately be seen as a factor undercutting the very legitimacy of the institution itself, for the aggressive building of images is always in direct proportion to the existence of possible arguments against those very images.

But why I am here is not the subject of this lecture. What *will* be at the focus of this lecture is the highly serious social game of political

This essay was first presented at the University of Bophuthatswana on the occasion of the Sol Plaatje Memorial Lecture in 1984.

images, the assumptions behind them, and how they are projected in an attempt to define reality.

II

Following the tradition of African-American autobiographical narratives of life under American slavery, the publishers of Sol Plaatje's *Native Life in South Africa* may have felt compelled to introduce to their readers, overwhelmingly white, this 'native' writer of 'considerable education and ability'.[1] Under the chapter entitled 'Who is the Author?' is a reproduction of the editorial of the *Pretoria News* of September, 1910. After a brief and fairly straightforward chronological account of Mr. Plaatje's history, the editorial goes on to evaluate in the following manner:

> Mr. Plaatje's articles on native affairs have been marked by the robust common sense and moderation so characteristic of Mr. Booker Washington. He realises the great debt which the Natives owe to the men who brought civilisation to South Africa. He is no agitator or firebrand, no stirrer up of bad feelings between black and white. He accepts the position which the Natives occupy today in the body politic as the natural result of their lack of education and civilisation. He is devoted to his own people, and notes with ever-increasing regret the lack of understanding and knowledge of those people, which is palpable in the vast majority of the letters and leading articles written on the native question. As an educated Native with liberal ideas he rather resents the power and authority of the uneducated native chiefs who govern by virtue of their birth alone, and he writes and speaks for an entirely new school of native thought. The opinion of such a man ought to carry weight when native affairs are being discussed.[2]

This evaluation gives us the impression of a newspaper sympathetic to the liberal view current at the time regarding the relationship between Africans and Europeans in South Africa. Specifically, that view was that Africans were acceptable as people on condition that they threw away their purported backwardness and accepted 'civilisation'. But then we can surmise from the special pleading tone of the editorial that this liberal view was generally unpopular in the European settler community. The newspaper was faced with the delicate task of pruning some over-vigorous branches of the political and social dispensation at the time, without appearing to be cutting down the entire tree.

Discovering in Sol Plaatje an intelligent, articulate, and accomplished African writer, the editor of the *Pretoria News* seeks to promote Plaatje as a symbol of what Africans might be, given a more intelligent, liberal atmosphere in South Africa. But since this is a risky task, the editor must devise a promotional technique by which to advance Plaatje while, at the same time, containing that advancement within strict limits of what was acceptable. The editor comes up with a technique of containment, the essence of which is to show that the likes of Plaatje, while making legitimate claims, are really not a threat to the white man. On the contrary, and more fundamentally, the likes of Plaatje are essentially on the side of 'civilisation'. After all, look, hasn't Plaatje displayed 'common sense and moderation'? Sol Plaatje 'is no agitator or firebrand, no stirrer up of bad feelings between black and white': in fact, he belongs to the same camp, as it were, as Booker T. Washington, that energetic, controversial African-American educator in the South of the United States, who was generally acceptable to whites as a leader with 'common sense and moderation'. Furthermore, isn't Plaatje grateful to the white men 'who brought civilisation to South Africa'? That is why Plaatje 'accepts the position which the Natives occupy in the body politic as the natural result of their lack of education'. Because Plaatje is 'an educated Native with liberal ideas', he has significantly moved away from his 'uncivilised' brethren, and singularly 'resents the power and authority of the uneducated chiefs who govern by virtue of their birth alone'. Plaatje now 'writes and speaks for an entirely new school of native thought'.

In short, isn't Plaatje wonderful? Isn't he just like us, white liberals? And so, if you can accept us, couldn't you accept him too? He's got blood like us. He is a new Native in our image: intelligent, articulate, educated, yet a 'good Native', really, who in the final analysis, knows his place.

We can see how an internationally positive editorial, steadfastly attempting to cultivate a certain image for Plaatje, seriously undercuts itself as well as its subject. Why is this so? Firstly, this liberal ideology is caught in the trap of language: it has not really freed itself from a language the vocabulary of which reflexively describes the prejudices of the time, which also undermine prevailing standards of what is acceptable or unacceptable. The essence of the problem is this: if we define success, for example, according to the standards and formulations of the oppressor, if we build buildings like him, if we plan our cities like him, if we teach our children like him, then we have, in a very fundamental manner, become the oppressor. He can even give us independence. And this is because we may not have been able to transcend oppression in its most insidious and dangerous ideological form: language and a complex of socio-cultural codes slowly legitimised over a period of time until they have become part and parcel of what is considered normal. In our attempts to call for freedom, we may, at the same time, be unconsciously prescribing our own containment. To return to the editorial, then, what we find there is the reflection of a relatively low level of self-critical awareness. This fact may be responsible for a certain tone of self-deceptive self-satisfaction, as well as the lack of a more penetrating theoretical understanding of the real dynamics of South African society.

The second reason why the editorial undercuts itself is that the liberal ideology displayed in it ascribes to itself a false universal validity. That is the reason for its tactics of containment. That is why it seeks to domesticate its potential allies by defining them in its own image. This attitude shows an inability to discover the essence of social conflict: the clash of material interests. The fact of the matter is that South African economic history has created over the last century or so, a vast class of workers which is black, on the one hand, and on the other, a powerful class of capitalists and their managerial functionaries, the overwhelming majority of them being white, together with a complex social range of beneficiaries whose claim to privilege is based on the white colour of their skins. That is the fundamental reality of the South African social formation.

No matter how much the editor of the *Pretoria News* can claim ideological consonance between himself and Sol Plaatje (admittedly, he is writing during the early though already decisive stages of that process), the real issues are more complex than that simple claim. Their interests can never entirely converge. Universality is a concept seldom free of class interest. In simple terms, failure to recognise this fact in the progress of history will make us party to that so-called Honourable Minister in the South African cabinet who when asked why Africans were so cruelly uprooted and resettled in those parts of the country now called 'national states' said: 'They like being moved'. Clearly, the man probably obsessively believed that the interests of the people being moved coincided with his own, never mind the bulldozers and the police. He had committed the fallacy of universalising his interests. Such ideological encapsulation has the effect of obscuring reality.

The truth of this position becomes even more glaring when we go on to read Sol Plaatje's book and examine his testimony. Plaatje constantly explodes the image created of him. Firstly, emerging as a much more sophisticated writer than a reader of the editorial would presume, Plaatje is a more conscious user of language, one more fully aware of its range of resources. He opens his prologue in the following manner:

> We have often read books, written by well-known scholars, who disavow, on behalf of their works, any claim to literary perfection. How much more necessary, then, that a South African native workingman, who has never received any secondary training should in attempting authorship disclaim, on behalf of his work, any title to literary merit. Mine is but a sincere narrative of a melancholy situation, in which, with

all its shortcomings, I have endeavoured to describe the difficulties of the South African Natives under a very strange law, so as most readily to be understood by the sympathetic reader.[3]

What we find here is a kind of tactical humility which is consciously undercut by the confident poise of language and style, and whose expressed reservations about its own merits assert the very opposite of inadequacy. When we think that Plaatje is fitting into the oppressor's image of the uneducated 'native', he explodes that image by assuming a contrary yet positive image himself. When the editor thinks that he has placed Plaatje firmly in his hands, Plaatje demonstrates that he possesses the capability to fly away. What Plaatje recognised in language is the dialectic of ambiguity, of understatement, literary tradition, and subtle, highly suggestive allusion and other similar things. Such an awareness of dialectic in language shows in Plaatje a potential ability to recognise a similar dialectic in the material transformation of history. Does he in fact go on to recognise such a dialectic? In another part of the prologue, Plaatje writes:

When Sir John French appealed to the British people for more shells during Easter week, the Governor-General of South Africa addressing a fashionable crowd at the City Hall, Johannesburg, most of whom had never seen the mouth of a mine, congratulated them on the fact that 'under the strain of war and rebellion the gold industry had been maintained at full pitch', and he added that 'every ounce of gold was worth many shells to the Allies'. But his Excellency had not a word of encouragement for the 200 000 subterranean heroes who by day and night, for a mere pittance, lay down their limbs and lives to the familiar 'fall of rock' and who at deep levels ranging from 1 000 feet to 1 000 yards in the bowels of the earth, sacrifice their lungs to the rock dust which develops miner's phthisis and pneumonia – poor reward, but a sacrifice

that enables the world's richest gold mines, in the Johannesburg area alone, to maintain the credit of the Empire with
a weekly output of 750 000 pounds worth of raw gold.[4]

Plaatje demonstrates here that he is aware of the class contradictions
inherent in the South African social formation. That is to say, he is
aware of the fundamentally exploitative relations that exist between
classes. The class that holds economic power controls the ideological
means by which the basis of their economic power can be given
political, moral, legal, and cultural legitimacy. In other words, they
control all the instruments for social definition. The essential task
of ideology in this situation is to hide the ugliness that accompanies
economic production, and to highlight the glitter of what is called
civilisation, which is spread like a layer of ice cream over all kinds
of ugliness. It is at the level of ideology that the attempt is made to
universalise class interests. Plaatje exposes the deception of ideology
in this situation.

For example, in the above passage, we can note several things
about the operations of 'civilisation'. We note the irony that the
appeal for more instruments of war and destruction are made 'during
Easter week', that Christian holiday which is supposed to be the
very affirmation of life. We note, too, that His Excellency the
Governor-General of South Africa brings his appeal for more shells
to a 'fashionable crowd' in Johannesburg. We note further, that His
Excellency congratulates, in essence, the wrong people: the non-
producers. The actual producers have been effectively obliterated
from the consciousness of the 'civilised'.

We can see, therefore, how the ugliness that forms the foundation
of western 'civilisation' in South Africa is effectively hidden from
view by the attractive glitter of Christian holidays, official government titles, city halls, fashions, and gold.

We cannot help but note, also, that the arbitrary parcelling out
of those largely barren parts of South Africa to Africans was the
result of the Land Act of 1913, the iniquities of which Plaatje exposed
before the world. In that exposure, he shows how the justifications

for this Act, leading to its full implementation today, were made in the most glowing terms in Parliament, so that the whole scheme could be seen as an impressive rational construct, the very best, politically speaking, that 'civilisation' could offer, while its underlying reality, the actual suffering of people, remained even up to today an indefensible obscenity.

Lastly, Plaatje is also aware of another mechanism of oppression aimed at obliterating the human essence of the oppressed in order to justify their brutal exploitation. Pointing out that he is not writing his book 'on behalf of the naked hordes of cannibals who are represented in fantastic pictures displayed in the shop-windows in Europe',[15] Plaatje seeks to emphasise the fact that he *is* writing on behalf of real people – not for the monstrosities existing in the minds of colonialists ever since Daniel Defoe conjured up Friday in *Robinson Crusoe*. Once you have denied the human reality of the oppressed, you can do practically anything you like with them. An essential condition of their continued oppression is their symbolic non-existence.

A few key conclusions emerge from our observations so far: firstly, Plaatje clearly does not 'accept the position which Natives occupy . . . in the body politic as the natural result of their lack of education'. That impression exists as a fiction in the mind of the editor of the *Pretoria News*. Secondly, Plaatje's attitude towards traditional 'uneducated' chiefs, as can be seen in the rest of *Native Life*, is not entirely dismissive. Thirdly, it is instructive that the editorial compares Plaatje with Booker T. Washington, whereas Plaatje implicitly appears to associate himself with W.E.B. Du Bois, whose book, *The Souls of Black Folk* Plaatje specifically mentions in *Native Life*.[6] This last point is worth pursuing further.

In the history of African-American literary and socio-political thought, *The Souls of Black Folk* has always been contrasted dialectically with Washington's *Up From Slavery*. These two books represent competing ideological positions with regard to the progress of the African-American struggle for freedom in the United States. The struggle, which begins from the universally accepted premise of the fundamental injustice of slavery, naturally demands confrontation with the abhorrent system. But the actual methods of confrontation always assume a dialectical difference which denies the actual struggle the desired consensus in the field of battle. Washington's method was tactical accommodation, what Du Bois called 'adjustment and submission', while the method chosen by Du Bois was radical.[7]

The difficulty with Washington's method is the problem of what is called 'working within the system'. It becomes very difficult to know exactly when *tactical* accommodation has become *actual* accommodation; when 'fighting within the system' has become an excuse for a willing participation in the system. Du Bois's method, on the other hand, has the advantage of keeping intact the ideological and analytical purity of the goals and methods of the struggle for liberation. Indeed, Washington's method of 'working within the system' cannot be successfully applied outside of the broad field of definition prescribed by the second method. The first method is meaningful only if it can be prescribed from within the ranks of the liberation movement. Beyond this, the essential advantage of the second method of radical confrontation is that it commands a vast field of creativity outside of the direct control of the oppressive system. The simple fact is that one can achieve more ultimately within the context of this method than within the other. Here the field of independence is beyond the easy manipulation of the system.

Finally, it can be seen from the foregoing analysis that most of the key assertions the editorial makes about Plaatje present in our minds a one-dimensional character who has no complexity to him. An essentially positive estimation of Plaatje, given the historical conditions existing at the time, in its attempt to make Plaatje an acceptable character, creates a picture that denies Plaatje a meaningful vitality. The editorial isolates Plaatje and places him outside of the dynamic and independent history of the African struggle. It puts him, through a largely unconscious manipulation, into a controllable tradition more familiar to the ideological inclinations of the liberal editor.

III

It may be asked why we have taken this long to come to the real subject of tonight's discussion? This delay was worth it because there is a fundamental lesson from the example of Sol Plaatje. It is the habit of mind displayed in his writings that has important implications for our topic. Firstly, Plaatje's approach to reality is rigorously empirical. This is probably a result of his career as a journalist. Plaatje comes across in *Native Life* as a writer who did not believe in hearsay evidence. He wanted to witness with his eyes the major historical events of his time.[8] Secondly, Plaatje does not come to hasty conclusions. This method is inductive. He piles up evidence until the situation presented condemns itself through the totality of oppression depicted. Thirdly, in his analysis Plaatje reveals an awareness that, in the kind of society created in South Africa, it is not only races that have been put into conflict, but also economic classes. Fourthly, through this analysis, Plaatje probes beyond the myths of what was considered 'normal' at the time. This ability to go beyond the surface of things is the single, most important attribute in Plaatje that has direct implications for our topic. Lastly, Plaatje is firmly placed in the genuine history of the struggle for liberation in South Africa. His role in that struggle has been that of methodical observer and interpreter.

While Sol Plaatje largely focused his critical attention on the oppressor, I would like us to attempt the opposite: to focus our attention on the oppressed themselves. I assume that the work of looking at the oppressor, of unmasking his claims, will continue to be done. That, it seems to me, is on the whole a much simpler task. The evidence of oppression, after all, is all around us to see. What is not so easy to understand is how that oppression *actually* affects the oppressed. How well do the oppressed really understand themselves in relation to the oppressor? How much do the oppressed understand themselves in relation to one another? These, it seems to me, are fundamental questions at this point in our struggle.

Basically, the problem is as follows. Because the educated section of the African population have traditionally assumed leadership in many areas of African life, particularly in politics, the question needs to be asked: have they interpreted realistically the actual desires of the masses they have set out to lead? Is it not possible that in the history of the struggle the leadership class has ascribed to the masses interests that were not the interests of the masses? Is it not possible that this false ascription has led to a fundamental confusion on the part of everyone as to what the struggle was actually about? In other words, in any society, there are actors and interpreters; there is popular culture on the one hand, and on the other, the formal culture which attempts to explain and to give ideological credence to popular culture at the highest conceptual level. It is this relationship between lived life and ideological conceptualisations of it that is fraught with problems. This relationship is the subject of the rest of our discussion.

IV

In any society, the makers of history, that is to say, those who bring about the actual material transformation of society, tend to be disproportionately more numerous than the interpreters of social transformation, that is to say, those whose business is to formulate theories of society in order to design more efficient social practices for the realisation of basic human needs: food, shelter, and various institutions of social control such as parliaments, churches, or schools. The interpreters of human history, in whatever branch of human endeavour, have always been faced with the task of designing theory out of social practice.

It is important to understand that the formulators of theory have an important role in the evolution of human society. This role is determined by the fact that human progress allows only so much random social experimentation, so much random exploration, so much social trial and error. In order to prevent perpetual random social experimentation, every society will reach a stage where it has to consolidate the existing accumulated social knowledge and, at the same time, create groups of specialists whose task it is to observe and experiment under more controlled, more disciplined conditions. That these specialists should constitute a minority is thus understandable.

Society, as a rule, strives constantly after more and more efficient means for ensuring its survival. In this task, the role of designated specialists is to work towards knowledge through the discovery of consistent patterns in the operations of both natural and social phenomena. Once they have discovered these patterns, they come up with a conceptual understanding of reality, which gives society a capability to deal with that reality more efficiently. For example, in the field of educational psychology, the Swiss Piaget, after observing children closely to discover how they actually learn, comes up with a theory of cognitive growth which states that, in general, children are unable to understand certain concepts until they have reached a certain level of mental growth. The practical implications of such a theory are that we can design a more efficient system of primary school education by producing relevant teaching materials for various age groups and levels of intellectual development. We can also design the most conducive physical conditions for the stimulation of mental growth. Here we have a theory of learning that results from a close encounter with experience yet makes that original experience more efficient and fulfilling.

The real point of these observations is to show the tremendous responsibilities that interpreters of society have towards the rest of society. Being few in number, they nevertheless do work that may have an impact far greater than their numbers. Their fundamental responsibility, therefore, is to promote, through their study of society and nature, the broad social interest to the extent that that interest has been accurately defined.

In the fields of history, political science, art, and general culture, the responsibilities of formal interpreters of human society become even greater. The discovery of consistent patterns, of real trends in social behaviour is a process that may require many years of study, before certitude can be reached. That is why an era cannot evaluate itself accurately. It is too involved with itself to be objective.

Momentary insights can easily and erroneously be accorded universal validity. The task of interpreters here is to come up with a method of observation and study that will yield high explanatory value. It is to aim at objectivity that will leave little room for wishful thinking in our understanding of history. Since human society is so complex, they must come up with theories of society that will attempt to encompass that complexity, yielding the highest explanatory value possible. One theory that has exerted considerable impact on our understanding of social history is based on the understanding that the progress of human history is determined by conflicting human interests regarding the control of such basic things as land, the production of food, the accumulation of wealth and the social use of it, and the regulation of various institutions of social control. According to this theory, the most compelling pattern in the progress of human history has been the emergence of the class struggle.

We have already seen how this method of looking at society was implicit, although in a rudimentary fashion, in Plaatje's *Native Life*. The nature of South African social formation and the prevailing ideological climate at the time made it impossible for Plaatje to follow his approach to its logical conclusions. And here can be found Plaatje's limitations. But it is sufficient to know that *Native Life* is a committed book, and that it is committed on the side of a large economic group against another smaller group. And the book shows a commitment that is based on a conscientious empirical understanding of the predominant social and political conditions existing at the time it was written. Plaatje was one of the few who, by virtue of ability and having found the time, made it his duty to observe, study and interpret.

Time does not permit me to be as empirically rigorous as Plaatje. But our starting point is that if one accepts the implications of the class struggle, as I do, then one ought to conclude that given the nature of the history of capitalism in South Africa, the African people, among whom the overwhelming South African working class population is to be found, is destined to be a subjugated people for some time to come unless the present dispensation is questioned at a fundamental level. It also goes without saying that if the African working class has been the material creator of the enormous wealth of South Africa, then a material arrangement and an ideological climate that validate their interest, are likely to be decisive factors in the creation of a new truly democratic and just society. It is the mechanisms by which this can be brought about that I shall now go into.

V

I shall attempt to discuss these mechanisms by looking at the state of African literature, particularly fiction, in South Africa. I focus on this particular field because it is my considered impression that our literature, as an art form, is remarkably backward in its general development. The forms of music, drama, and the visual arts, particularly sculpture, are advanced in comparison. Literature appears not to have found a place in the development of contemporary African culture in South Africa. Instead, in groping for this place, literature has located itself in the field of politics. And it has done so without discovering and defining the basis of its integrity as an art form. Its form therefore, has not developed, since to be fictional or poetic was to be political. There are reasons for this, of course, and we shall try to get at them in due course. And perhaps we can arrive at these reasons by looking at the relative success of the other art forms.

Casual students of the history of African music in South Africa soon realise that *mbaqanga* music is reaching ever greater heights in its development. A significant influence in this development is the contribution of such musicians as Makeba, Masekela, Mbulu, Ngwagwa and Semenya. Their contribution, however, should always be looked at in the context established by their forerunners – the Elite Swingsters, Spokes Mashiyane, Lemmy 'Special' Mabaso, Zakes Nkosi, the early Dark City Sisters, and several other groups. The popularity of these musicians was never in doubt. But from the early single 'Grazing in the Grass', through the albums *Union of South Africa* to *Techno-Bush*, Masekela has helped to push *mbaqanga* music to unprecedented heights. So have Semenya and Letta Mbuli.

The popularity of these musicians in the medium of *mbaqanga* is not in doubt. A similar development can be noticed in the case of drama and sculpture. Why is this so?

Mbaqanga music is most manifestly rooted in location culture. It represents the kind of successful adaptation that took place in the course of the proletarianisation of the African peasant in the new urban industrial centres of South Africa. African music was given a new range of expression by the concertinas, guitars, violins, mouth organs, and later brass instruments and the piano.[9] In time, these instruments were completely domesticated and became part and parcel of urban musical culture. The development of *mbaqanga* music, therefore, is firmly based in the urban popular imagination. Its legitimacy is inseparable from the spontaneous, self-consciousness of African popular urban culture. This culture is beyond the easy manipulation of the apartheid culture. The recording companies no doubt attempted, with a large measure of success, to commercialise this music. But that in itself was a recognition of the firm popular foundations of the music. They have, on the whole, been able to recognise inventiveness that not only ensured sales but also continuously added new musical dimensions to the music.

What our exiled greats such as Masekela and Semenya have accomplished was to create an advanced musical culture of formal and deliberate experimentation with *mbaqanga* music. Working at the highest level within the popular tradition, these musicians enriched the tradition in unprecedented ways. The effect has been to internationalise the music as a specific contribution of South Africa's locations to the musical culture of the world. Today, progressive experimentation is the order of the day, as the musical practice of such groups as Sakhile can testify.

A similar situation can be observed in township drama. In attempting to shed light on the career of Gibson Kente, Robert Kavanagh observes:

> Kente's success had been built on a foundation of excellent but uncontentious popular musical theatre and dramatically

expanded after 1973 when he discovered that political protest theatre was even more commercially rewarding – at least initially. Kente's motives for joining the new wave of radical theatre in the 1970s . . . almost certainly included genuine feelings of nationalism occasioned in his own case by the frustrations suffered generally by black businessmen in the urban areas and the realisation that his increasingly young audience was growing more militant and demanding stronger stuff. Whatever his reasons, he found himself in a position in which he was subject to a serious contradiction. His plays had to cater for the increasing militancy of his mass audience, yet as a successful businessman both confrontation with the state and civil disorder in the black areas – let alone a popular revolution – constituted a threat to his financial interests. The contradiction is reflected in his play, *Too Late*.[10]

Even more specifically, Kavanagh notes how Kente's earlier plays exploited popular township cultural behaviour:

None of Kente's earlier plays raised social and political issues. Instead the plots exploited what is called 'human interest'. Kente created characters and set them in situations which either amused or moved the audience to pity or terror. His music was the principal instrument for developing the emotional potential of these situations. If the plays had a message at all it was 'every cloud has a silver lining' or that's life.[11]

What is evident in these analyses is how Kente, an obviously talented theatre craftsman, attempted to come up with plays that were in tune with popular sentiment. His imagination was grounded in popular experience. He enabled his audience therefore to see itself on stage and to reflect, in no matter how rudimentary a fashion, on what they saw. We see also, how Kente was forced to take into consideration the popular political climate in the location environment, although that kind of preoccupation could potentially jeopardise his commercial interests. He had to grapple with all the attendant problems of staying in tune with the demands of his community.

It seems clear then, that the success of drama and music is connected with the relationship between popular culture and progressive experimentation with that culture at the level of form and content. Everybody sings, and everybody acts in one way or another. But African culture in the townships has also produced, as is the case with all societies, a specialist group of musicians and dramatists who are professional, and therefore, formal interpreters of that culture in its popular aspects. A very close dialectical relationship exists between the actors and the interpreters: the interpreters begin from the mass actors, and in turn, advance the consciousness of the mass actors. Mao Tse-Tung analyses the relationship between popular culture and the theoretical articulation of that culture in a manner that clarifies clearly the issues involved here:

> The people demand popularisation and following that, higher standards month by month and year by year. Here popularisation means popularising for the people and raising of standards means raising the level for the people. And such raising is not from mid-air, or behind closed doors, but it is actually based on popularisation. It is determined by and at the same time guides popularisation.[12]

We see here the dialectical relationship that has already been discussed above.

A neat theoretical formulation of these ideas is necessary, and here we make use of the ideas of another scholar. The definition of popular culture, contends David Coplan, should take into consideration:

> the social bases of popular culture and the relations of cultural production in particular. Popular performance derives its

vitality and ultimately its entire meaning from the quality of public participation. Ideally, popular art should arise out of relationships between artists, supporters, audiences, and other participants who form a segment of a larger community of experience and interest among working people. The key factor is the relationship between social forces and the immediate producers of public art. Thus it matters very much whether the performance activity grows from the 'bottom up' as an organic, autonomous, effort to formulate and dramatise community concerns: or whether it is distributed from the 'top down' by cultural entrepreneurs, mass media interests, or even the government. We might make a distinction here then, between 'popular' culture and 'mass' culture, based on the degree of alienation of cultural labour. This distinction must be operationalised as a continuum, not a dichotomy.[13]

According to this formulation, it is clear that the success of drama and music in the townships has much to do with the fact that the professional practitioners of these art forms did not abandon the class basis of their respective art forms. The effect of their work has been to promote and to consolidate the cultural values of the working class through artistic media. Working within the scope of this culture, they have not found it easy to distort it. Their representation and interpretation of popular culture takes place within the context of a genuine dialectic which stands to improve and advance that culture as it develops in history.

What is the problem with our literature – our fiction and our poetry? Here, I think, we are entering into a very difficult and complex field. But a serious attempt must be made to seek answers. Essentially, the problem seems two-fold. Firstly, it has something to do with the nature of the written word itself. How do we acquire it? Secondly, there is the question of the kind of socio-historical circumstances which determine the extent to which many people can use the skills of reading and writing, and why they may need to use those skills. Specifically, why do we learn to read and write?

And when we have learnt to read and write, what social and economic factors permit us or do not permit us to continue to develop those skills?

To deal with the first problem, it should suffice for our purposes to note that reading and writing are skills that have to be acquired under special circumstances. Normally, we have to go to school in order to acquire these skills. The acquisition of these skills, therefore, is a conscious act of education. You do not learn how to read and write without being aware of the fact that you are actually acquiring an education. The relationship between these skills and the concept of education has been firmly established historically. If these propositions are valid ones, and we can only permit ourselves to leave them as propositions at this stage, then we have to pass on to the second issue: why we often find we have to acquire these skills, and how they can continue to be of use to us.

The concept of education in South Africa, as was the case in the rest of colonised Africa, has always been linked to its colonial origins. Education was provided in order to usher Africans into the light of western civilisation. So education, in the manner in which it was understood and largely continues to be understood, implied African absorption into another culture. The first colonial task was to create an initial reading and writing elite that would be a symbolic representation of the successful attainment of civilisation. In time, the reading and writing elite became a minority social class whose material interests largely correspond to colonial interests. This meant that, from the onset, the necessary adaptation of the written word into an instrument for promoting an evolving popular culture – an adaptation parallel to that which took place in music – was to be almost indefinitely delayed. This meant also that the popular consciousness of formal modern education as organised social advancement was never fully developed.

However, it should be noted that although this elite shared the material interests of their colonial promoters, they continued to suffer as a result of the colour of their skins. In their fight to overcome racial discrimination they needed to enlist the African working class as allies. They therefore began to use the written word to express political demands, propagating in the process the idea of using the pen as a sword. This led to a situation in which by virtue of their ability to read and write, they ascribed to themselves the leadership role of writing on behalf of the oppressed. In time, the written work came to be associated with the task of making political demands. The written word, therefore, in the history of the African struggle, became associated with political exposition. But it is exposition which has been dominated not by the masses but by a minority group within the African population.

The coming of Bantu Education in the early fifties served to consolidate what was already a socio-political reality: the lack of an adequate education for the mass of the African population. Although the African was to get an education, it was only so that he could be a better servant who could understand simple instructions and read simple messages. The African could not be allowed to develop reading and writing skills beyond these basic demands. In like manner, Bantu Education further entrenched the position of the African elite as literate interpreters, who nevertheless had no real educational base within the larger African community. The result was that the African masses were effectively alienated from the written word. The written word has never been allowed to become an essential ingredient of modern African mass culture. This whole situation, of course, is much more complex than this outline can show, and certainly requires more study.

The result is that today we have two social forces which control social attitudes towards the written word, and both these forces operate from the 'top down' rather than from the 'bottom up' in their attitude towards the African working class. Firstly, those identified above as 'cultural entrepreneurs, mass media interests, or even the government'. They produce a range of cheap picture story magazines, glossy 'sophisticated' magazines like *Pace*, sensational journalism, and publishing in the African languages that is dominated by vast Afrikaner publishing houses with links to the government. All these interests produce a mass reading culture that defines, respectively, the written word as simple language accompanying pictures; the written word as urban sophistication; the written word as sensationalism; and the written word as ossified rural culture of the so-called Bantustan policy of the government.

The second social force that influences urban attitudes to the written word is the African elite we have already identified. For them, the written word, as we have seen, is politics. The effect of these two groups, therefore, is to produce a 'mass' culture as opposed to a 'popular' culture as we have defined these terms earlier. Their efforts to represent and interpret mass culture do not emerge from an intimate interaction with popular experience. Their attempts at representation and interpretation are more likely to be fraught with distortions, misunderstandings, and misinterpretation.

As far as literature is concerned, the picture can become clearer now. The written word has never been seriously looked at as an aesthetic medium, as a medium for articulating the serious concerns of the working people. Only recently, for example, with the efforts of such organisations as the South African Council for Higher Education (SACHED), are we beginning to see serious attempts to turn the written word into a serious means expressing popular concerns, or to domesticate the written word so that it becomes part and parcel of the modern mass culture in a creative manner. Only on this basis has the written word the potential to be a serious aesthetic medium in South Africa.

The relative success of autobiography in South African literature is interesting here. Autobiography steers a course that is very close to exposition. It is in fact what one might call expositional narrative. And in the specific conditions of South Africa, personal testimony can only be meaningfully understood as political testimony. So that autobiography has also consolidated, in the final analysis, the notion of the written word as politics.

In conclusion it can be said that in general, the writing of fiction and poetry in South Africa has been influenced by an ethos that defined the written word as politics. Consequently, African writers have tended to approach their task with a severely limited view of the possibilities of the written word. When they assert like the literate elite discussed earlier, that they are writing for the masses, they are essentially correct, for they are not writing *with* the masses. They are writing from above rather than from below. They come armed with the task of educating the masses about politics. In the process, they give us instruction without social explanation. What is the solution?

Here I would like to return to the example of music. It is interesting to note the subject matter of the lyrics of popular *mbaqanga* songs. These musicians build their songs around a variety of human problems such as marriage, infidelity, relationships between women and their in-laws, going to work on cold winter mornings, jealousy, crime (occasionally we come across a philosophical piece on the importance of music, or the wonders of nature, and similar subjects). The tone is usually of open rebuke, or satire; of moral judgement, wise instruction, or advice. Always at the centre of these concerns is a deep ethical interest, that is to say, an interest in what ought to be done in order to promote an harmonious society. We have also noted how Kavanagh identified a similar interest in Kente's work. Essentially, Kente seemed concerned about problems of social instability as a result of pervasive crime in South African black townships.

These kinds of popular preoccupations have tended to exasperate the political, literate elite which includes writers. Why do the workers not demand more explicit, more direct political content from their popular composers? The exasperation is no doubt a result of an inadequate understanding of the social content of political discontent. Popular political interest revolves around the need to find solutions to practical social problems of various kinds. Hence the ethical interest. The mass of the people are busy trying to bring about a normal society in spite of oppression. It must be realised that this concern for a normal and ordered society, no matter how rudimentary, is probably the only genuine base from which working class culture can project a truly autonomous definition of an ideal society. Writers should not think that such mundane concerns are trivial. They provide the only meaningful context, the only base from which a new society can be created. In other words, while fighting for the future we must think about how we are actually going to live.

Revolutionaries, for example, are not always busy fighting. They are also busy loving, jilting each other, being envious of one another, and so on. The point is to work during the actual progress of struggle, towards the kind of society, in which such specifically human problems can best be managed and turned towards creative ends. In other words, the struggle is not just a matter of fighting, it is also, perhaps more fundamentally, a matter of creating new social values. And you can only create new social values by concerning yourself with real society in its various forms. So, rather than despising the song on jealousy and faulting it for lacking politics, we must begin from the social reality of the song and then attempt to explore its ethical meaning. Seen in this way, the social context of politics is an infinitely complex yet challenging phenomenon. Society is the very content of politics: that is the lesson of popular experience.[14]

A study of the stories that appeared in *Drum* in the fifties may be instructive in this regard. *Drum* began as a 'Jim comes to Jo'burg' magazine which attempted to help the rural 'native' adjust to the stresses of urban life and still come out alive and dignified. It was designed for the sophisticated who, at the same time, were not supposed to lose their rural simplicity. The early stories were on the relationship between rural life and urban life, with the latter coming off at a disadvantage. But the pattern soon changed. The urban readers demanded stories that reflected the only life that they now knew best. The popularity of *Drum* increased when it became an urban magazine.[15]

Urban life offered more possibilities for survival. The reader's imagination was constantly challenged. The stories reflected the excitement of that challenge. But it is also important to note that the creative writing in *Drum* existed side by side with creative journalism: the journalism of Henry Nxumalo, for example. There was a creative consonance between political interest, social excitement, and imaginative vigour. The detective serials of Arthur Mogale, for example, were immensely popular. They showed daring, resourceful thinking, sophistication, personal confidence, all of which reflected the social state of mind of an urban people that wanted to make strong demands on its environment. The protracted bus boycotts of the fifties, for example, can only be meaningfully examined against an explanation that included this kind of background.

The writers of the fifties are surprisingly silent over questions of political relevance in their writings. Perhaps there was an intuitive confidence in the knowledge that resistance to oppression was a complex multifaceted undertaking, such that the political was understood in an inclusive, holistic sense rather than in the narrow sense of party politics. Political resistance, in other words, can also be understood as total communal self-assertion. In the world of fashion, beauty contests, sports, of the 'first African this . . . the first African that', of organised crime, we have social data of tremendous significance. And it lacks 'relevant seriousness'. We must begin from the social fact of this data rather than from a moralistic or radical idealism which wishes that people were better than they actually were, without accepting the responsibility of beginning with and from what they actually are. The writers of the fifties, in this regard, were more in tune with the organic popular perceptions. The task is to reflect the outward features of the popular imagination while vigorously subjecting them to inner critical scrutiny.

There is something else important that writers need to understand. Here we return to our discussion of the relationship between the skills of reading and writing and the act of education. A significant dimension to the understanding of fictional practice by the writer is the knowledge that reading and writing are consciously directed activities. The written word and active consciousness are very closely related. The full educational benefits of reading are to be derived from the knowledge that the relationship between fiction and real life is not a one-to-one relationship, but a relationship by analogy. As a result, each act of reading must necessarily result in interpretation, and the act of interpretation is discussion of the text either with oneself or with others. The world of fiction presents itself to us as one which requires discussion. Indeed, readers have always discussed popular stories. Real fiction, therefore, is creative discussion of real social issues.

The possible solution to the problems of our fiction would appear to lie in the following: our writers must constantly assess their level of understanding of society.[16] Secondly, they must enhance their understanding of the nature of their art and its medium of language. Thirdly, they must cultivate a total interest in their community. Fourthly, they must take an interest in the spread of literacy in the working class community. Lastly, their definition of what constitutes politics must be as inclusive as possible. Only in these ways can literature, the art of the written word, take its rightful place in the development of a progressive culture. The written word, being so central to the experience of the modern world, and the vast possibilities for intellectual development that it offers, must be brought to the centre of modern popular consciousness. The path of real and fundamental liberation lies in that direction.

VI

I would like to return to the larger issues that began this discussion. I do this in order to emphasise the point that the role of fiction or art in the history of struggle should never be overestimated. Artists, writers, and musicians should never have an unrealistic view of the ultimate social significance of their work. Fiction can never replace politics in the total scheme of things. But having said that, I want to make some observations about the history of the larger struggle, since there are theoretical matters that unify committed writing with revolutionary politics. I merely want to mention the problem and leave to progressive historians and political scientists the task of providing the necessary explanations.

A casual view of the development of our struggle seems to show that the African political movement has been most successful at those moments when the formal political articulators of the mass political will fully identified themselves with the expressed interests of the African workers. The ICU in the twenties, for example, is a case in point. Its power appears to have grown at a time when the accepted ANC leadership was ideologically out of tune with real popular interest. Indeed, there are several times when the masses appear to have taken to the political field unassisted, often surprising the formal political will. The strikes of 1945 and 1973 are cases in point.

If these observations are valid, and they are based so far on casual assessment, then they would point to a serious recurring weakness in the history of the movement. I would identify this weakness as a lack of sustained consonance between the popular will and formal political analysis. It would appear that formal political analysis, not founded on the empirical realities of township life, has been theoretically undeveloped. Such political images as emerge from the available theory appear to have come from the minds of the literate political elite. There is the question here of the credibility of representation.

One wonders, therefore, how effective has been the attempt to raise the standards of popular political analysis. To what extent has the attempt been made from within? Certainly, the writers of fiction appear not to have been significantly influenced by consistently serious and genuine political theory based on the kind of empirical rigour displayed by Plaatje in his *Native Life*. One still waits for an organic theory of the South African struggle from the active cadre either within or outside the country since 1960: the kind of theory that would rival, in its depth of explanatory analysis the work of Cabral, Nkrumah, or of any of the great revolutionary thinkers of the world, who have attempted to theorise and articulate the popular interest at the highest formal level. This entire matter, however, calls for its own separate and full treatment. Here, I am merely trying to voice a question posed by the thought that serious progressive writers cannot really subsist in an ideological desert.

I would like to conclude, in the spirit of my address, by directing my final words at those who are students of this institution and others like it. Indeed, I am addressing myself also to those educators who are battling with serious questions regarding the relevance of their work. It is our task, all of us, to constantly ask why this institution (and others like it) is here: to ask to what extent the popular will was taken into consideration at the time it was built. If we find that the interests of the suffering masses were not considered seriously, then we must be prepared to conclude that perhaps this institution might be part of a complex of formidable forces perpetuating oppression. A house without a foundation. To remedy such a situation, we would have to ask what can be done to bring the interests of the popular will to the centre of our intellectual concerns. We have to look at the syllabus; we have to look at the structure of authority (how democratic is it?); we have to look at the teaching methods (how innovative and progressive are they?).

It should be clear why I am here today. I decided, according to my thinking, that given my theoretical understanding of the key issues affecting us in South Africa, what I wanted to say in the quest for a new and vigorous approach to the fundamental problems of liberation, was much more important than where I was going to say it. I can hope that the persistent and fearless pursuit of truth will be the key guiding principle behind our intellectual work, to enrich the theoretical content of our struggle *wherever that struggle is taking place*.

NOTES

1. *Pretoria News*, September, 1910. (Quoted in Solomon T. Plaatje, *Native Life in South Africa, Before and Since the European War and the Boer Rebellion*, [Kimberley, New York: Tsala ea Batho, The Crisis, 1917], p.9.)
2. Ibid. p.10.
3. Solomon T. Plaatje, p.11.
4. Solomon T. Plaatje, p.16.
5. Solomon T. Plaatje, p.15.
6. Solomon T. Plaatje, p.16.
7. W.E.B. Du Bois, *The Soul of Black Folk*, (U.S.A.: Fawcet, 1961), p.48.

8. For example, see Solomon T. Plaatje, pp.58–90.

9. David Coplan, 'The Emergence of an African Working-class Culture', in *Industrialisation and Social Change in South Africa: African Class Formation, Culture and Consciousness, 1870–1930*, S. Marks and R. Rathbone (eds.), (London: Longman, 1982), pp.359–60. Coplan notes:

> Among the agents of urban social and cultural transmission were the so-called Coloureds, who brought two-hundred-year-old traditions of professional musicianship and the institution of the illegal, private drinking house, or *shebeen*, with them from the Cape. Through Coloured influence and the experience of labour and transport-riding for Afrikaner farmers, western 'trade-riding' instruments, including the guitar, concertina, violin, auto-harp and mouth-organ, became popular among migrant and farm labourers as well as among urban workers. These instruments and many urban stylistic influences were incorporated into traditional music and dance culture.

10. Robert Mshengu Kavanagh (ed.), *South African People's Plays*, (London: Heinemann AWS, 1981), p.xxiv.

11. Robert Kavanagh, p.xxv.

12. Mao Tse-Tung, *Selected Works*, Vol.III, (Peking: Foreign Language Press, 1967), p.83.

13. David Coplan, 'Popular Culture and Performance in Africa', in *Critical Arts: A Journal for Media Studies*, Vol.3, No.1, 1983, pp.1–8.

14. E. Obiechina in *African Popular Literature: A Study of Onitsha Market Pamphlets*, (Cambridge: C.U.P., 1973) notes:

> The Onitsha Market literature is concerned with the business of living. It is about young men and women who are intensely alive and who, because they are so, have problems arising from the complexities of modern life. Most of those at whom the literature is directed have had only a superficial contact with modern ways and are in need of guidance and help if they are to cope with them. (p.18)
>
> The writers of these pamphlets are obviously in tune with needs of their community. We can see here, the potential for the written word to be totally domesticated so that through it, the popular intellect can attempt to deal with its complex environment in historically, socially, and culturally familiar terms.

15. See Anthony Sampson, *Drum: An African Adventure and Afterwards*, (London: Hodder & Stoughton, 1956).

16. Chidi Amuta in 'Towards a Popular Literary Culture in Nigeria', *Critical Arts*, Vol.13, No.1, A.83, pp.55–64, observes:

> [the] question of roles for the Nigerian (or African) writer is an exhausted controversy in African literature. What has not been sufficiently examined are the appropriate strategies for actualising these roles. The crucial challenge in this respect is, to my mind, that of whether the Nigerian bourgeois writer – who is ultimately the 'sensitive point' of *his class* – can reach the popular without committing class suicide. (p.61)

5

❖ ❖ ❖

THE ENGLISH LANGUAGE AND SOCIAL CHANGE IN SOUTH AFRICA

The current political context appears to have left its mark on the manner in which this conference itself was conceived and organised. I am thinking here of the attempts on the part of the organisers to consult various individuals and groups, anticipating that a diversity of interests can be accommodated in the various discussions that will take place in the course of the conference. Such conduct is, no doubt, fully in keeping with the demand of the oppressed of this troubled land for full democracy in the conduct of every aspect of the country's life.

Yet, well-meaning though these attempts may have been, it is essential, at such times, that we exercise a state of vigilance that will enable us to express tactical reservations – if only to ensure that all relevant issues have been brought to the surface, so that we can make pure motives even purer. The fact of the matter is that, viewed from the angle of those towards whom the hand of friendship is being extended, such democratic largesse can become an unintended trap. For example, it should never be forgotten that behind the hand of friendship is the presence of the Academy's solid institutional history: a history that has left its mark on habits of thought in the

This essay was presented as the keynote address delivered at the Jubilee Conference of the English Academy of South Africa; Johannesburg, September, 1986.

literary culture of this country. Consequently, when such an organisation seeks urgently to respond to certain pressing exigencies of history it will do so from the assumed validity of its organisational base, and such a base would tend to dictate a strategy of benevolent containment and encapsulation in order to maintain, expand, and to exert influence. Under such circumstances, the organisational base itself might even appear to be a negotiable factor, when in fact, it is not. This is because it is usually so firm as to make it almost unthinkable for the organisation to consider the possible strategy of self-sacrifice so that it could be absorbed into a new and necessary, if seemingly threatening, dispensation. This is to suggest that when a centipede curls itself into a protective stance, it remains a centipede.

Now, the subject of central concern to this conference is the evolving place of English in Southern Africa. It makes perfect sense that since the English Academy's central interest is the promotion of the English language, the Academy should devote special time to this matter just at that moment when South Africa finds herself compelled to seek new directions into the future. Indeed, it has become the sign of the times that any organisation that regards itself seriously should engage in the mandatory exercise of re-evaluation at this crucial time in our history.

In keeping with my opening remarks, it is pertinent to note that some renowned thinkers, who are native speakers of English, have observed over the years the development of the English language around the world. Observing the spread of English throughout the world, and how that phenomenon has meant that, with the advance of years from the era of colonialism, the development of English in various parts of the world has taken forms that have gone beyond the control of the native speakers, they have concluded that English is no longer the exclusive property of its native speakers. No less an authority than George Steiner commented back in 1965, that:

> The great energies of the language now enter into play outside
> England . . . African English, Australian English, the rich
> speech of West Indian and Anglo-Indian writers, represent a

complicated polycentric field of linguistic force, in which the language taught and written on this island is no longer the inevitable authority or focus.[1]

In South Africa, our own Professor Guy Butler has remarked in a recent article that 'twenty million blacks will use English for their own interests and ends, without worrying much about the views of less than two million ESSAs (English-Speaking South Africans)'.[2]

There are at least two possible responses of the native speakers of English to this seemingly inevitable process. They may celebrate, in the spirit of international linguistic democracy, the birth of new languages based on the English language; or, they may descend into fits of anxiety, firstly over the purported mutilation of their language with the possible attendant loss of intelligibility, and secondly, over the fear of the loss of influence.

Unfortunately, it is the latter response that has won the day. Beginning from a positive and open-minded acceptance of reality, this latter response has triggered off concerted efforts by metropolitan English speaking policy makers to effectively stem the strong tide of history. This has entailed attempts to weave a web of containment around this spontaneous, world-wide transformation of the English language so that English can continue to serve various kinds of metropolitan interests; interests which may have very little to do with the concerns of those who, out of specific needs arising from their own forms of social interaction, have to fashion a new language for themselves.

Practically, this need to maintain control over English by its native speakers has given birth to a policy of manipulative open-mindedness in which it is held that English belongs to all who use it provided that it is used correctly. It is assumed, of course, that it is the native speakers who will determine the standards of correctness. In other words, you really cannot control what will eventually happen to English in the hands of non-native speakers; but then you can control it. This is the art of giving away the bride while insisting that she still belongs to you.

That this latter tendency predominates should not surprise anyone who attempts to ask some ultimate questions, for this tendency will then be found to be perfectly consistent with the history of English and, later, American imperialism. The much vaunted traditions of English and American democracy have promised an attractive world of 'freedom and opportunity' to all those who would enter that world. Yet, many of those who entered, mainly as colonial subjects, soon discovered that the newly promised freedom was premised ultimately on the subject's unfreedom. The colonial subject had to give up much of what constituted his own sphere of freedom. And so, the very concept of freedom came to be standardised, in the same way that technology and business culture were standardised, according to the specifications of imperial powers.

Indeed, the history of the spread of the English language throughout the world is inseparable from the history of the spread of English and American imperialisms. This fact is important when we consider the place of English in formerly colonised multi-lingual societies. The imposition of English effectively tied those societies to a world imperialist culture which was to impose, almost permanently, severe limitations on those countries' ability to make independent linguistic choices at the moment of independence. We have since heard much about how practically all of those countries ostensibly took the 'pragmatic' decision to choose English as the *lingua franca*. How can we fail to notice that an historically predetermined 'pragmatism' has been transformed, by the metropolitan culture, into an act of choice, on the part of subject cultures, and then praised as the very essence of wisdom? How can we fail to note that the supposed decision makers were, structurally speaking, captive native functionaries of the imperial powers? In reality, the functionaries merely responded to the call of necessity at a given point in time: the necessity of limited choices. After all, when you want to use an electrical gadget in Africa, hadn't you better purchase a plug that meets specifications standardised in the western world?

It is not too difficult to see how English as a language became tainted with imperial interests at that time in the progress of western imperialism when the need for the standardisation of technology prompted the need for the standardisation of language. In fact, I would hazard a guess that the very concept of an international or world language was an invention of western imperialism. In any case, the language chosen was destined to be English, with French fighting hard for the title. Consequently, the spread of English went parallel with the spread of the culture of international business and technological standardisation. From there, the jump towards the standardisation of international thought becomes easy to make. Today, the link between English and the western corporate world is stronger than ever.

As far as South Africa is concerned even Professor Butler notes how 'major international corporations are pouring money into black schools, frequently with the specific aim of improving English'.[3] Beyond that, the British Council too, continues to be untiring in its effort to keep the world speaking English.[4] In this regard, teaching English as a second or foreign language is not only good business, in terms of the production of teaching materials of all kinds (a service business sector that increases the numbers of possible consumers of British and American commodities throughout the world), but also it is good politics. The Commonwealth, after all, is an alliance of historically captive users of English.

Now, English-speaking South Africans are, inevitably, heirs to the history of the English language. In South Africa, they constitute an English language outpost that is expected to do its historical duty towards the imperial heritage of the language. For example, in the article already alluded to, Professor Butler, while altruistically denying to the English-speaking South Africans an ethnic interest in the English language, since the language really belongs to all, evokes that interest when he asserts that 'White English-speakers must enlarge their constituency; they can only do this by enlarging the influence of their language'.[5] This necessarily follows from how Professor Butler imbues English-speaking South Africans with a patriotic duty to help teach English in South Africa and to teach it well. 'The importance of good models of spoken and written English cannot be over emphasised,' asserts Professor Butler. Consequently, 'English should be taught effectively as it used to be in the old mission schools, in which there were always devoted English-speaking models'. Indeed, they were devoted! Furthermore, it is 'particularly important that future teachers of English in black schools should be educated and trained in institutions where a significant number of the staff have English as a mother-tongue or are highly proficient speakers of it'.[6] Clearly, we can see here a permissive attitude that goes hand in hand with the prescription of standards. Let us call it a prescriptive open-mindedness.

All of which goes to indicate that the role of English in South Africa is a matter the complexity of which goes far beyond the convenience and correctness of its use, for that very convenience, and that very correctness, are, in essence, problematic. The problem is that recourse to them is fraught with assumptions. Recourse to them begs fundamental historical, cultural, and political questions on the assumption that everyone knows what issues are at stake. But, in fact, we cannot assume the validity of premises that have not themselves been scrutinised carefully. This latter tendency not to be critical about premises is pervasive in South Africa at the moment when all kinds of scenarios of the future are being drawn up in the hope that the oppressed will be dazzled. This problem is so important that we need now to look at the problem of English from a national context.

If we look at the testimony of many white organisations on the question of change in South Africa, we shall immediately discern a pattern of thinking and attitude that seems to typify what the average white person, the traditionally privileged, thinks about the central problems of change. These organisations fall into three general categories.

First, we have organisations whose interest in a future dispensation is determined almost entirely by their economic interests. For example, I am thinking in particular of an organisation such as the Association of Chambers of Commerce of South Africa (ASSOCOM). Recently, ASSOCOM commissioned Professors J.A.

Lombard and J.A. du Pisanie to provide 'academic help' in drawing up an ASSOCOM memorandum called 'Removal of Discrimination Against Blacks in the Political Economy of the Republic of South Africa'.[7] This memorandum was to be prepared for 'submission to the Cabinet Committee on the political future of Urban Blacks'. The memorandum is important not so much for what it says, but for the package of assumptions that provide an uncompromisingly non-negotiable context for the memorandum's submissions.

Central to the memorandum's position is the following starting point:

> Believing that REFORM should be governed by (a) adherence to sound PRINCIPLES of statehood and (b) EVOLUTIONARY rather than revolutionary changes, it is proposed that the acceptable basic elements of the existing order be identified, recognised, and extended.
>
> It is suggested that these basic elements are to be found in the COMMON LAW of South Africa, with particular reference to the norms governing (a) personal freedom, (b) freedom of property and contract, and (c) personal culpability. A DECLARATION OF RECOGNITION by all negotiating parties of these norms would be a necessary condition for further progress in negotiations. To these three common law norms should be added a formal recognition of (d) the basic rules governing the maintenance of a sound national currency and (e) the principles governing the right to tax.
>
> It is further suggested that the PHILOSOPHY BEHIND THE COMMON LAW NORMS which currently govern the basic character of the private enterprise economic system of South Africa, be extended to form the basis for the new POLITICAL STRUCTURES within which blacks will participate on equal terms with other citizens of the Republic of South Africa.[8]

Behind the evident posture of reasonableness in this passage are pitfalls that can trap the unwary. The memorandum, for example, offers a negotiating position while subtly positing, at one and the same time, non-negotiable principles. The sign posts of these non-negotiable factors are there: '*sound* PRINCIPLES of statehood'; '*acceptable* basic elements of the *existing order*'; '*sound* national currency'. Behind such words as 'sound' and 'acceptable' are firm assumptions about what is desirable. They hide the ideological anxieties of their users. Behind such seemingly objective virtues of efficiency are such unstated declarations that 'we must preserve our way of life as we know it'; 'all those who are reasonable and privileged enough to think like us will see the value of our position'; consequently, there is an implied strategy that 'we may have to educate the opposition'. In this latter regard, the last paragraph in the above quotation is more explicit: the 'basic character of the private enterprise economic system of South Africa' must be left intact. The legal philosophy behind that system must be 'extended' so that its specifications can also cover black people. This implies that the concept of 'human nature'[9] may need to be distributed more widely to include black people. Indeed, the memorandum refers to black people as 'the prospective black citizens of the Republic'.[10]

It seems to me that the more appropriate title for the memorandum should be 'The Protection of Capital in a Rapidly Changing South Africa'. In this regard we may not fail to notice the significance of the fact that ASSOCOM is an 'Incorporated Association not for Gain'. It may not be 'for gain', but ASSOCOM is clearly interested in creating a climate that can maintain conditions for maximum gain for its members. Fundamentally, the qualification regarding gain is a kind of deceptive propriety.

The second category of organisations includes those groups which have attempted to produce all kinds of scenarios for the political future of the country. They include, of course, such groups as the Progressive Federal Party, and, yes, today, the Nationalist Party. The latter has produced a set of scenarios that have led to the kind of constitutional tinkering that has resulted in the Tri-cameral Parliament. Of course, nothing illustrates more dramatically than this parliament, the futility of reform politics. Indeed, these acts by the Nationalist Party should properly be called, 'the modernisation of the methods of maintaining white domination'.[11] That, is the hidden definition of 'reform'.

More significantly, however, is how some highly influential organisations in this second category are to be located in universities where they draw upon the aura of objectivity associated with university research. Perhaps none is better known than Professor Schlemmer's ill-fated Institute of Social Research based at the University of Natal, Durban. There is much intellectual tinkering that takes place in the context of such institutes which derives its authority not necessarily from the ideologically biased findings of research (although the intellectual practitioners involved will proclaim their objectivity), but from the backing of those findings by an intellectual hegemony based on the rituals of research, statistical data and evaluation, the presentation of findings at seminars, and the dramatic press release. The politics of academic research is no more glaring than in such a situation. Always lacking is the sense of genuine conviction in the necessity of a future that accommodates the intuitions of the oppressed, for the oppressed themselves have been reduced into being a mere 'factor of analysis' among other factors. Nevertheless, when the history of South Africa is finally updated, it may be found that the country has never had so many political theories thrown up for discussion.

Lastly, diverse cultural interests have issued a challenge to the future which involves the need to open up cultural and educational centres to all races. Missing in these admirable acts of goodwill is an accompanying need to alter fundamentally the nature of cultural practice itself. It is almost always assumed that, upon being admitted, the oppressed will certainly like what they find. The opening up of white private schools, for example, is a good illustration of the strategy of containment through absorption. Where there has previously been the absence of freedom, the mere exercise of making facilities available may easily be mistaken for the presence of freedom. That way, a dominant hegemony that has been in existence is left intact as it gains more supporters from among the ranks of the oppressed.

What is common to all these diverse interests? It is the unquestioned, non-negotiable, primacy of western civilisation and its spectrum of values embodied in what has been called free enterprise and the special kind of democracy based on it. There is no doubt that the influence of the West in South Africa is vast, that it rubs off on all segments of South African society, and that it is destined to continue well into the foreseeable future. Its active defence, though, is largely a matter of habit, indicative of an entrenched and largely uncritical manner of thinking about the quality of life on the part of those who have benefited vastly from what has been called 'the South African way of life'.

Unfortunately, for the vast majority of South Africans, western civilisation has not glittered as it has for those who brought it here. For the majority of the oppressed, the experience of western civilisation has largely been the experience of poverty, malnutrition, low wages, mine accidents, police raids, selective justice, and a variety of other similar negations. Consequently, this majority has not been, as it were, hegemonised to any great extent. For example, thanks to apartheid, they are so largely untouched by much of the discourse of western political philosophy that, even at the popular level, buzz words and expressions such as 'human rights', 'free enterprise', 'human dignity', 'self-determination' and other standardised elements of political vocabulary have not been absorbed to the extent that they would figure prominently in the people's subjective experience of political language. On the contrary, the relatively few members of the political majority who have been aware of such vocabulary are those who have experienced it as applying to the privileged whites. Thus 'human dignity' was the dignity of whites; and 'human rights' were the rights of whites.[12] Hence, black people's experience of western civilisation in general has been premised on their exclusion from its perceived advantages, except when, for purely functional or utilitarian reasons, their participation was sought. This kind of functional participation is even more evident today, when it is required in order to legitimise white South Africa's perceptions of 'acceptable' change. So that even at that crucial moment of historical transformation, the oppressed have to experience themselves as tools.

In a well known poem, Agostinho Neto sums up the relationship between most of Africa and western civilisation graphically:

Western Civilisation
Sheets of tin nailed to posts
driven in the ground
make up the house.
Some rags complete
the intimate landscape.
The sun slanting through cracks
welcomes the owner

After twelve hours of slave
labour.
breaking rock
shifting rock
breaking rock
shifting rock
fair weather
wet weather
breaking rock
shifting rock

Old age comes early

a mat on dark nights
is enough when he dies
gratefully
of hunger.[13]

From the foregoing discussion, it should be clear that much of the talk about reform and change, from the point of view of white South Africa in general, is premised not on what the whites of South Africa may have to unlearn, but on what black people, those 'prospective citizens of the Republic', need to be speedily introduced to so that they can become 'responsible' citizens of the future; so that they can become westerners in black skins. In a nutshell, the entire ideology of reform is based on the 'humanisation' of the oppressed according to the specifications of South African capital, which, itself, is governed according to the specifications of the international corporate world.

The practical aspects of this modern form of colonial 'pacification' imply the implementation of modern principles of business management. In the same way that the scientific attitude in eighteenth and nineteenth century Europe influenced the entire spectrum of European thought, today, the dominance of international monopoly capital has bequeathed to the world 'principles of management'. Such an approach to reality has made it habitually difficult for corporate authority, as well as those influenced heavily by that authority, to discern the fundamental causes of human disaffection. 'Management principles', in situations where the desire for freedom is as deep as it is among the oppressed in South Africa, are applied like the analgesic that is habitually administered to kill a headache where rest would have ensured a more permanent cure.[14]

For the present, the challenge before the spectrum of white South African interests subscribing to the ideology of reform, is the 'management' of the irreversible demand by the oppressed for liberation. This 'management' attitude began with the Sullivan Principles at the work place, and was extended to the need for the creation of an African middle class in the context of the larger society. Mirrored in this strategy is the desire to 'manage' African aspirations through the intended effect of substituting the technicalities of civic responsibility (the 'opening up' of white business areas for blacks, the ninety-nine year lease, the creation of Community councils, abolition of apartheid at the work place, employee housing and other worker benefits, etc) for the fundamental desire for freedom.

Clearly, the 'management' attitude leaves largely uncomprehended and untouched the reality that the call of the oppressed for freedom is premised on the total subversion of the social 'biology' of South African repression.[15] This kind of desire for liberation is based on a complete understanding and recognition by the oppressed, of the fact that the white ideology of reform is based on the white's 'biological' need to maintain a sense of social and individual well-being that is based on a structure of needs validated by the white's oppression of others. The greatest pathology of such a social system is the blunting of the humanistic vision and the constriction of the intellect resulting in the death of the social conscience of the beneficiaries of the system. Consequently, any reformist prescriptions for the future, emanating from the oppressor, are bound to be an inextricable part of the culture of repression. On the other hand, for the oppressed, the pathology has prevented the realisation of their human potential. As a result, the oppressed, as the direct victims of such a society, have no vested human interest in maintaining it. This is because the structure of social needs nurtured by such a society is incapable of ensuring a new, more humanistic sensibility that can be the only liberating condition for the birth of new men and women in South Africa.

The inherently subversive quest for freedom by the oppressed of South Africa is even more evident today where their erstwhile demand merely to be allowed to participate in the various structures of government has clearly given way to an insatiable desire to create: to create comparable structures on the basis of a new human sensibility. Where much of the activity of political resistance up to the sixties was not premised on a far-reaching, fundamental critique of the nature of government and economic arrangements for the production and distribution of national wealth, later, especially since the end of the sixties and throughout the seventies, and mainly under the impetus of the Black Consciousness Movement, many black organisations, primarily of a professional nature, were established as *alternatives* to the system: students, social workers, lawyers, doctors, journalists, workers, and other professional sections of the black community, established alternative organisations of various kinds in both urban and rural areas. They did this in order to create institutions that were independent of those established by white power; ones which could effectively articulate and project the concerns and interests of the oppressed.

However, there have since been further significant developments. What we are beginning to witness now, is a further shift towards the establishment of alternative structures at *grassroots level* in various communities in the townships as well as in some rural areas. The establishment of these grassroots organisations is, no doubt, a response to the intensification of the struggle and the deepening of experience resulting from it. For example, the call for rendering the townships ungovernable has given way to the need for their governability, only this time on foundations *rooted in the experience of the people themselves*. Unfortunately, whites are not present while these significant changes are taking place. The same is the case with industry. Yet, what is happening in the townships is bound to have a tremendous impact on the way government will be organised, how the education system is going to be altered, and on the way in which relations of production in the corporate world may have to be rearranged. Here, new forms of democratic participation are being created out of the practical experience of township life.

This situation must present South African radical intellectuals with their greatest challenge thus far: the emergence of new forms of democracy, of new ways of social thinking, will require not a condescending and manipulative attitude of management, but a deep understanding; the kind that should lead to a radical codification of social thought which results from new forms of social practice. Specifically, some of the challenges may manifest themselves in the following directions.

Firstly, it would appear that relations of power within the African family, particularly in the townships, appear to have undergone a tremendous transformation. For better or for worse, there is an increasing tendency towards parent/child consultation. To what extent, then, will this development affect the quality of family life, and in what directions? Whatever the case may be, the practice of democracy in the home is bound to have a marked effect on its practice in the immediate neighbourhood, in the first instance, and then, ultimately, in the entire country.

Secondly, one space which will definitely be affected is the working place. Industry may be compelled to take into account the

114

emergent needs of the evolving African family. What adjustments may need to be made in concepts of production; in the relationship between the factory, the workers in it, and the community those workers come from?

Thirdly, since the aim is not to reproduce old bureaucratic structures of government which over the years have habituated the mentality of repression, emergent grassroots democracy may have to be elevated right up to the level of national government. In this regard, what forms of participatory democracy will emerge, which will express the spirit of the quest for a new morality?

In the fourth place, the remoulding of the educational system toward one that will inculcate these emergent values and speed up, at the same time, the production of skilled and educated Africans at all levels of social and economic activity, is at the root of the new day.

Also central to the need for a new education is the recognition that apartheid culture has been a cultural disease that has deformed whites themselves. As it has been suggested above, the disease has ingrained in them the habit of experiencing their well-being in terms of their oppression of others. For this reason, it cannot be taken for granted that whatever white South Africans have to offer is inherently valuable. Their blue prints for the future may be tied up with social 'biological' needs that can only be met under the old negation. Everything is going to be subjected to the most rigorous scrutiny. In this regard, the re-education of whites should constitute a crucial area of education, for indeed, the educators themselves need to be educated. For example, white children by and large are not participants in the making of the future right now. Tragically, where they participate they come in as soldiers to smother the dreams of their peers. Whatever vision of society determines their actions, it is dead to the future. The social virus of apartheid can be seen to reproduce itself even at that very moment that fundamental change is called for. The white polity, even as it watches with culpable indifference, the physical killing of black children, is busy killing the souls of its own children. Of what use can these children be to the future?

In the fifth place, in concert with new needs, it may be essential to work out new technological priorities.

Finally, what kind of means need to be devised to facilitate the rapid yet creative improvement of life in the rural areas?

This has been a rather lengthy digression from the question of language. But, in fact, the issue of language should become clearer from the broad social perspective that has just been drawn. From this perspective, one can go on to evaluate the state of any aspect of society. But since our interest, at the moment, is in the English language in South Africa, we shall necessarily proceed to focus on it specifically.

Basically, I think that we cannot afford to be uncritically complacent about the role and future of English in South Africa, for there are many reasons why it cannot be considered an innocent language. The problems of society will also be the problems of the predominant language of that society, since it is the carrier of a range of social perceptions, attitudes, and goals. Through it, the speakers absorb entrenched attitudes. In this regard, the guilt of English then must be recognised and appreciated before its continued use can be advocated.

For example, Professor Butler, in his very persuasive essay, makes several statements which reflect traditional views on the validity of the English language in multi-lingual societies, particularly those in Africa. Here is a list of statements made by Professor Butler. They indicate the depth of the problem as I see it:

1. The English language is of vital concern to all South Africans. (p.164)
2. The English pose no political threat to anyone. Their language, however, is wanted and needed by all. (p.165)
3. Blacks have not forgotten the quality of those old mission institutions; and they are more determined than ever to have command of English. (p.168)
4. English, unlike the other languages in South Africa, is not 'an own affair' of the ESSAs. It is everybody's affair, because

it is indispensable in a way that our other languages are not. (p.169)

5. In expressing his support for a unitary system of education in which English may have to be the sole medium of instruction, Professor Butler makes a remarkable statement: 'Thought, like money, has no colour'. (p.169)

6. White English speakers must enlarge their constituency; they can only do this by enlarging the influence of their language. (p.172)

7. The 'democratic tradition, and . . . the English language, these are deep in ESSA birthright and tradition, and are open to all South Africans'. (p.172)

I shall not discuss these points in turn because I think the context in which they could be examined has already been spelt out earlier in this discussion. The inherent limitations of these statements will now be obvious. But I shall briefly sum up my response. We could begin with the remarkable statement that 'Thought, like money, has no colour'.

The remarkable thing about this statement is that it is true. But even more remarkable, for our purposes, is that it is incomplete. It should also be added that 'thought, like money, is linked to economic and social class'. For example, it has been shown that the corporate world in the United States, controlling vast sums of money, also effectively controls thought in that country: a fact which renders problematic the much vaunted concept of freedom of speech there. Thought, in the public domain in the United States, is canned thought, often selectively siphoned off from solid research and thrown at an impressionable public by sides contending for social, political, and economic dominance.[16] It is this canned thought that is then exported to the rest of the world through advertising, through corporate business English, through scientific gadgetry and its accompanying technical English, and through the political wisdom of the Voice of America. How could Professor Butler miss this phenomenon?

117

Of course, one does not want to give the impression that the world community uncritically accepts this kind of American onslaught on the international mind. But in countries where there are constituencies linguistically and culturally tied to American ideals, we should not be blamed when we insist on a rigorously critical kind of vigilance. It is at this point that we return to Professor Butler's call to ESSAs to show their patriotic duty in helping to 'spread their constituency' through the teaching of English. How can they spread their constituency without, at the same time, spreading their social vision through their language? Central to this vision, for example, is their 'democratic tradition'. Does this tradition include the kind of grassroots democracy that is flowering in the townships of South Africa at the moment? The implicit ideology sustaining Professor Butler's social and political vision definitely excludes this new phenomenon. Indeed, the link between thought and money is often fraught with intrigue!

I do not mean to suggest a mechanical one-to-one relationship between language and society, but I do want to suggest that before we declare English to be our unquestionable national language, we must be critically open-minded about several possible eventualities.

Firstly, South African English must be open to the possibility of its becoming a new language. This may happen not only at the level of vocabulary (notice how the word 'necklace' has acquired a new and terrible meaning), but also with regard to grammatical adjustments that may result from the proximity of English to indigenous African languages.[17]

Secondly, the teaching of English will have to be freed from the functional instruction of corporate English. A dangerous off-shoot of this corporate approach to the teaching of language is to be discerned in the SABC(TV) programmes of language instruction. The programmes are designed to teach whites selected African languages. Below is a typical teaching segment.

The aim of the lesson was to teach the question, 'where are you going?' in SePedi. Three whites each meet an African whom they ask in SePedi: 'where are you going?' The first African is a messenger who replies that he is going to the post office. The second one is a domestic servant who replies that she is going to the store, and the third one, a worker dressed in overalls, replies that he is going to some similar place of work. The point about these lessons is that seldom do the segments carry situations in which blacks and whites meet as equals. The situations are often ones which involve employer (white)/employee (black) relations. Remarkable about the segments is the functional context of language use. Clearly, the lessons are not designed to promote meaningful communication between humans; rather, they are designed to enable whites to make better use of their black workers. Thus, the psychological approach to language learning is flawed from the word go. No doubt, though, the SABC is convinced that it is 'bridging cultural gaps'.

There is yet another revealing aspect to the situation just described: it is that structurally speaking, the colonial relationship that existed between European and African cultures in South Africa is duplicated in the relationship that is being perpetuated between English and Afrikaans on the one hand, and African languages on the other hand. Where African cultures in the colonial context held, for imperial cultures, only an exotic anthropological interest, now, in the South African context, African languages hold a mainly functional, manipulative interest. They are a means towards a more efficient use of African labour.

The above example of language teaching by the SABC typifies the context of learning that characterises the traditional teaching of English to Africans. What may need to be emphasised is that if the recognition that English belongs to all who use it is more than academic, then in multi-cultural societies, English will have to be taught in such a way that the learners are made to recognise themselves through the learning context employed, not as second class learners of a foreign culture, or as units of labour that have to be tuned to work better, but as self-respecting citizens of the world. The idea of teaching English through the exposure of second language learners to English culture, should be abandoned. If English belongs to all, then it will naturally assume the cultural colour of its respective users.

Thirdly, in promoting English in a multi-lingual society, there is a danger that it may become increasingly difficult for us to make a distinction between English and education. At a certain juncture, education appears to have become synonymous with the acquisition of English. That being the case, a fracture between the acquisition of knowledge and the acquisition of English must be brought about. This is in the obvious recognition that the sphere of human knowledge is much wider than any one language can carry. Corporate English appropriates knowledge by equating it with the mere acquisition of language. That English may be spoken universally, does not imply that it carries the sum total of the world's wisdom. The sooner the oppressed of South Africa know that, the sooner will they appreciate the immense freedom of choice before them.

Fourthly, it may be said that there are aspects of English that are not tied to any manipulative interest: literature and the world of learning in general, for example. That may be so. But these considerations are seldom at the centre of the need to spread the hegemony of English today. Promoting a foreign language in another culture seldom reaches, for the vast majority of the members of that target culture, beyond the merely functional. That is to say, English is an international language, but it is international only in its functionally communicative aspects. For the rest of the time, indigenous languages fulfil the range of needs that English similarly fulfils for its native speakers. From this point of view, the functional acquisition of English, in a capitalist society such as ours can further reinforce the instrumentalisation of people as units of labour. So it is conceivable that the acquisition of English, precisely because the language has been reduced to being a mere working tool, can actually add to the alienation of the work force. Indeed, in the same way that grassroots organisations are meant to protect people from the oppressive impersonality of the state, indigenous languages can be a refuge from the manipulative impersonality associated with corporate English language acquisition.

At the centre of the problem, in fact, is the educative function itself. The humanisation of the educative function is a dire need, since South African society still has to produce a viable home-grown humanistic ethical tradition. From the word 'go', modern education in South Africa was tied to material accumulation. The pattern of rampant capital accumulation, set in the era of Cecil Rhodes, meant that the ability to found economic growth on the sound basis of a home-grown ethical culture was severely limited. That ethical culture, particularly for the ESSAs, especially in their moral stance towards the oppressed, became, instead, no more than humanitarian politics. And it is there, possibly, that we have the origins of that protective benevolence towards the oppressed, associated with that community. It is that persistent attitude that still wants to rescue the oppressed from ignorance through the vehicle of the English language.

We have come a long way from my introductory comments. They were not intended to be a direct criticism of the Academy as such. Rather, they were designed to be an analogical approach to my central thesis that an uncritical open-mindedness, in this case expressed as the promotion of the English language, can be a dangerous form of encapsulation. Beyond that I am certain that I have not exhausted this topic. The aim of this paper was to seize the opportunity to present and formulate the problems from the perspective that I have adopted. I can only hope that I have been sufficiently provocative to provide something for the participants of this conference to discuss and debate in the discussion sessions to follow.

NOTES

1. Article in the *Listener,* 21 October, 1965. (Quoted in *The Critical Evaluation of African Literature,* Edgar Wright [ed.], [London: Heinemann, 1973], p.3.)
2. Guy Butler, 'English in the New South Africa', *The English Academy Review 3,* Johannesburg (1986), pp.163–76.
3. Guy Butler, p.166.
4. Recently, the British Council began marketing, on behalf of the BBC, a package of audio-visual instructional materials called *Television English.* This package offers, among other things, 'interesting collections of carefully selected excerpts from

121

BBC TV programmes about a wide range of topics including: British life and customs, traditional crafts, medicine and health, new inventions, British institutions, history, people at work, fashion and clothing, leisure activities, food and drink, British countryside, music and art, buildings, British humour'.

Furthermore, the package is meant for 'intermediate to advanced learners of English around the world who

* are interested in seeing and learning about aspects of British life, culture, technology, humour, history, etc.
* would like to watch BBC television programmes in English and learn how to follow them.
* want to study the English the British use when talking to each other using current words and idioms'.

5. Guy Butler, p.172.
6. Guy Butler, p.173.
7. See J.A. Lombard and J.A. du Pisanie, 'Removal of Discrimination Against Blacks in the Political Economy of the Republic of South Africa', a memorandum for ASSOCOM, No.3, 1985.
8. Lombard and Du Pisanie, p.i.
9. Lombard and Du Pisanie declare that the 'market economy is the product of human nature and the politico-economic system patronising the market economy is based on a more realistic and consequently superior understanding of human nature'. (p.17)
10. Lombard and Du Pisanie, p.15.
11. See Heribert Adam, *Modernising Racial Domination*, (Los Angeles: University of California Press, 1971).
12. See note 9, above on the need for the extension of the economic-legal attribution of 'human nature' to black people.
13. Agostinho Neto, in *Accents*, M. Chapman and T. Voss (eds.), (Johannesburg: Ad. Donker, 1986), p.186.
14. For an extensive and most revealing analysis of this manipulative social attitude of modern corporate America see, Joel Kovel, *The Age of Desire*, (New York: Pantheon Books, 1981).
15. See Herbert Marcuse, *An Essay on Liberation*, (U.K.: Pelican Books, 1972). Note Marcuse's use of the term 'biology': 'I use the terms "biological" and "biology" not in the sense of the scientific discipline but in order to designate the process and the dimension in which inclinations, behaviour patterns, and aspirations become vital needs which, if not satisfied, would cause dysfunction of the organism. Conversely, socially induced needs and aspirations may result in a more pleasurable organic behaviour. If biological needs are defined as those which must be satisfied and for which no adequate substitute can be provided, certain cultural needs can "sink down" into the biology of man. We could then speak, for example, of the biological need of freedom, or of some aesthetic needs as having taken root in the organic structure of man, in his "nature", or rather "second nature"'. (p.20)
16. See Noam Chomsky, 'Thought Control in the USA: The Case of the Middle East' in *Index on Censorship*, Vol.15, No.7, July/August 1986.

17. Herbert Marcuse, pp.41–3, Marcuse shows how the struggle for liberation also takes place in the field of language itself. See also Mothobi Motloatse (ed.), *Forced Landing*, (Johannesburg: Ravan Press, 1980). Motloatse is very forthright:

> We will have to *donder* conventional literature: old-fashioned critic and reader alike. We are going to pee, spit and shit on literary convention before we are through; we are going to kick and pull and push and drag literature into the form we prefer. We are going to experiment and probe and not give a damn what the critics have to say. Because we are in search of our true selves – undergoing self-discovery as a people.
>
> We are not going to be told how to re-live our feelings, pains and aspirations by anybody who speaks from the platform of his own rickety culture.

6

❖ ❖ ❖

TOWARDS PROGRESSIVE CULTURAL
PLANNING

Peter Horn opens an essay of his with an observation pertinent to the subject of this paper.

> It is not true to say that there is no culture of the oppressed: but it is true to say that, where the oppressed are forcibly separated from their own political and cultural organisations, the influence of the media on the consciousness of the oppressed is much greater than in those countries where they create and distribute their own information through their own media.[1]

This observation reminds me of an analogous situation, involving a particular individual experience, in which Ariel Dorfman describes the transformation and awakening of a poor woman from one of the slums of Chile. While this woman, very much under the influence of the kind of media Peter Horn alludes to, had previously insisted on her reading diet of escapist 'industrial products of fiction',[2] something was to happen to her during the time of Salvador Allende's

Keynote address at the Conference on *Writers from South Africa: Culture, Politics and Literary Activity and Theory in South Africa Today*, October 30, 1987, Harris Hall, Northwestern University, Evanston.

125

brief presidency, that changed her attitude completely. Dorfman first makes a general observation to the effect that when a people attempts to liquidate centuries' worth of economic and social injustice, when they begin to gain a sense of their dignity as a nation, what is really at stake, what really inspires them, is an alternate vision of humanity, a different way of feeling and thinking and projecting and loving and keeping faith. And a different future.[3]

He then comments on the specific case of the woman from the slums:

> That woman from the slums was being shoved, poked, awakened. And while she was in that turbulent, searching stage, what she needed was a parallel interpretation at all levels of what her situation, of what the world, was. Not just a political explanation of why things were one way and how they might be transformed, but channels for expressing the joys, the doubts, the anxieties that come when people who were previously powerless begin to have some say in their existence. What she needed was a new language.[4]

How is this relevant to our discussion of culture and politics in South Africa? If we define culture broadly, as Horn and Dorfman clearly seem to do, then we shall appreciate the extent of the South African problem in terms of the perspective from which I'm going to attempt to look at it. A useful point of departure is Marek, Hromadka, and Chroust's description of culture in their UNESCO document on cultural policy in Czechoslovakia. They write that culture as a social process is an entire, internally structured system, in which we usually distinguish two aspects: material culture (sometimes denoted by the term 'civilisation') and spiritual culture. The term 'material culture' is usually applied to the material results of human work, as for instance to machines, technology, buildings, settlements, the mode of sustenance and clothing, the objects of everyday use. The term 'spiritual culture' is usually applied to an aspect of the cultural process which is oriented to the human soul, which creates and forms a man's intellect, ideas, feelings, ethical and aesthetic values, attitudes and behaviour; cultural values influence among others man's psychology and mode of living, and represent in principle the material results of human findings and knowledge in science, art and in the sphere of social standards.[5]

Now, the racist system of South Africa has systematically denied the oppressed majority any meaningful opportunity for creative involvement in the entire arena of cultural practice. It is not only that obstacles have been placed in their way in the fields of writing, painting, music, and the other arts, but also that, specifically, they have had no say whatsoever in the socially organised planning of society. They have had no say in the planning of their communities; in the designing and the building of the houses they live in; in the making of the clothes they wear; in the making of decisions regarding the safety of food, cosmetics, and medicines; in the determination of research priorities in science and technology; in discussions regarding the devaluation of the national currency; in the establishment of banks; in the formulation of agricultural policy; in the establishment of prisons, mental asylums, and hospitals; in decisions regarding the transportation of goods and people; in decisions to demolish old historical buildings, or to build museums. Characterised in these specific ways, political deprivation is given a concrete social, cultural form. What this suggests is that the oppressed were effectively denied the opportunity and the sovereign right and experience to create a complex human civilisation. This picture should serve to indicate the enormous task of reconstruction ahead, which will be undertaken in the attempt to enable the oppressed to discover a new, rich and very complex social language of their own.

One major consequence of this situation is that over the decades, the condition of sustained and brutal oppression has placed the burden of organised, organic cultural expression on political resistance. But, because of the relatively weak capability of the oppressed to deploy vast material resources to challenge their oppression, much of their means of resistance was dominated by the rhetorical articulation of political grievance. This means that the armory of resistance became largely abstract, not in a pejorative sense, but in the sense that the struggle became more and more a matter of articulating injustice and declaring goals. All the more then could the system deploy an array of ideological weapons (the media, for example), to influence the perceptions of the oppressed, since about three-quarters of the terrain of battle was effectively uncontested. The oppressed did not have an army of industrialists, engineers, architects, scientists, and a host of other professionals with whom to contest domination with the entire range of material culture, and thus, with a practical sense of the interconnectedness and organic unity of organised social activity.

Within this terrain of ideological conflict, two major approaches to the question of cultural resistance have dominated discussion. The first one I will call the restorative approach in which attempts were made, and are still being made with remarkable success, to reveal and restore to the oppressed the history of their cultural practice. Because the culture of the oppressed as a whole was, and continues to be, the target of imperialism, one of the major ways by which imperialistic intervention was justified was to deny the existence of this indigenous culture. Consequently, for example, when literature, virtually at gunpoint, as well as under the influence of the emergent market place of capitalism, and the implications for social organisation and control which this new system entailed, became synonymous, in our case, with English literature, and civilisation with western culture, then the culture of the oppressed as they had lived it before their domination, effectively ceased to exist. Amilcar Cabral puts it this way:

> History teaches us that, in certain circumstances, it is very easy for the foreigner to impose his domination on a people. But it likewise teaches us that, whatever the material aspects of this domination, it can be maintained only by the permanent and organised repression of the cultural life of the people concerned. Implantation of domination can be ensured definitively only by physical elimination of a significant part of the dominated population.

In fact, to take up arms to dominate a people is, above all, to take up arms to destroy, or at least to neutralise and to paralyse their cultural life. For as long as part of that people can have a cultural life, foreign domination cannot be sure of its perpetuation. At a given moment, depending on internal and external factors determining the evolution of the society in question, cultural resistance (indestructible) may take on new . . . forms, in order fully to contest foreign domination.[6]

In response to this kind of onslaught on culture, the call for restoration was made by Kwame Nkrumah, among others, back in the early sixties when he declared:

In the new African renaissance, we place great emphasis on the presentation of history. Our history needs to be written as the history of our society, not as the story of European adventures.[7]

But such a call was not new. Similar calls pre-date Nkrumah's call by several decades. Writers such as Tiyo Soga, Sol Plaatje, and Mangoaela, quite early in the modern struggle against imperialism, were already producing committed literature partly with the intention of preventing the total loss and destruction of African culture. But then, a conspiracy of silence, as a result of the culture of imperialism and racism, prevented the publication and distribution of such works. They virtually ceased to exist. Consequently, the work of such writers had to be resuscitated. That is why in recent times, heeding the call of decolonisation, many African historians have shed much revealing and liberating light on the history of our continent. Similarly, literary historians have brought to the surface a rich body of African literature which, only yesterday, was never ever thought to exist. This kind of resuscitative work should and will no doubt continue well into the future, as all oppressed communities in South Africa have suffered from the concerted silencing of their cultures.

It can be said, then, that the work of restoration, was designed to put before the minds of the oppressed the historical image of a legitimate and well organised social life. That is to say, an image of a civilisation built by their ancestors. This was done in order to suggest that the organised social strivings of the past, could be repeated.

The other approach to this question of cultural resistance has concerned itself with analysing cultural practice, particularly with regard to the arts, in terms of either its emotional or intellectual effect on society. Here the emphasis is on the capacity of cultural activity to influence social behaviour in the fulfilment of specific social objectives. Taking the particular example of literature, we immediately become aware of the extensive terrain covered by this approach in terms of the relationship between literature and society. How should writers reflect society? Should they write novels, short stories or poems? What should they write about? Who should they write about? Who are the readers of their books? What are the class origins of writers, and what are their positions on political issues? What is the relationship between a writer's political convictions and his work? Where should writers publish their work, and how best can their work be distributed? How do we train more writers? What are the levels of literacy in society? Exactly how do literary works impact on social behaviour? The questions are many and often difficult to answer. But they are constantly being grappled with by writers themselves, by professional critics, as well as by all kinds of people interested in literature. Much of the discussion of literature will almost invariably centre around any one of the questions posed.

Today I would like to pose yet another question. In the re-construction of society, what progressive societal role do we ascribe to cultural practice? How do we free ourselves from notions of culture that are tied to the ethos of oppression? When we probe a little further into the question we will note that it is not only cultural action itself that is under scrutiny, but also the kind of institutional arrangements created for the practice and promotion of cultural activity. Specifically, what would be the progressive attitude towards theatre halls, opera houses, cinemas, sports fields, concert halls, libraries, art galleries, museums, schools, universities, research institutes, the civil service, the institutions of commerce and industry, and a host of other facilities created for the purpose of promoting broad cultural activity. However, since the field is so vast, I shall limit my discussion to the narrow field of the arts, in the interests of both brevity and clarity.

Of course, I cannot pretend to have answers to these questions. Perhaps the current phase of the struggle has to assume a much firmer organisational form in terms of the necessary institutional-isation of progressive ideas. For example, to what extent does the answer lie in the successful consolidation of the concepts of street committees, people's courts, people's education, and other emergent alternative grassroots forms of social organisation? Clearly then the question one is asking is in essence a political one, and one which is fraught with implications for social action, since political objectives ultimately derive their legitimacy and efficacy from the success of practical and creative social action. It does mean then, that clarity of political objectives is fundamental.

The starting point for all of us is the uncompromising demand for democracy. This democracy will necessarily assume forms that take into account the history of our oppression. One visible factor of this history has been our enforced silence. This enforced silence also affected communication among ourselves, thus blunting our intellectual growth.

Hence our hunger for knowledge; our hunger for speech; our hunger for constructive social discussion; our hunger for the ultimate right: the right to determine the future with our minds and with our hands. Much of our energy will be turned in that direction. One way through which our voice can be heard is the way of art, and since we seek a consonance between all creative social activity on the one hand, and the collective political will on the other hand, the social relevance of art will have to be defined in the context of that search.

Confronted with concerted pressure from the oppressed, the South African government is seeking to find ways of accommodating the aspirations of the oppressed without giving up effective power. The technique is to persuade the oppressed that the existing structures of social and political organisation are open to them on condition that the ways in which they function are not altered. So it is with all the other benefits of science and technology. In other words, the seemingly objective efficacy of science and technology is a matter beyond debate. The resulting policy of reform then, is based on the premise of the objective validity of the oppressors' own cultural practice and the results thereof. This reasoning, of course, is fundamentally flawed.

I would like to attempt a preliminary analysis of this problem by first quoting at length from the work of Joel Kovel, a radical American psychiatrist, who provides us with a useful analogy. The book is called *The Age of Desire*, and the relevant chapter, 'The Administration of the Mind':

> Consider a simple and seemingly neutral example: the necessity for traffic lights in a big city, 'rationally' timed to ensure the flow of traffic. Traffic 'naturally' tends to be chaotic, since the human organism cannot regulate the great power of the automobile. Enter a bureau of traffic and a traffic engineer who impersonally studies the flow of traffic, figures the problem out mathematically, and sets up a system of lights. And behind him enters the traffic police to impersonally enforce the law which, by saying one has to stop for lights, caps off the whole process of traffic rationalisation. Now everyone is happy, for no one can force his way across intersections without paying a penalty. Even the tycoon, who can buy his way out of anything, pauses before the impersonal majesty of the traffic law, partly to forestall nuisance, partly out of concern for the dangers inherent in violating the law. People readily internalise the discipline of traffic signals. The most unruly lout will, in the vast majority of instances, stop at the red and go at the green. Even psychotics readily obey.
>
> But when we focus on the rational need for bureaucratic intervention into the social complexity of traffic, we can lose

sight of the reality behind the complexity. The flow of traffic in a city is primarily determined by the needs to get workers to and from the workplace and consumers to and from the stores; and secondarily, but equally deeply, determined by the need to keep markets expanding for corporate behemoths who fatten on traffic: oil companies, automobile manufacturers, road builders, etcetera. Therefore, the complexity of traffic is a direct function of the exigencies of capital accumulation. And capital accumulation can never relent; its every success only feeds its chaotic tendencies. The more 'efficient' the traffic lights make this system at one level, the more uncontrolled they will make it, and the society defines it, at another level, the level of pollution, of energy squandering, inflation, techno-logical unemployment, mechanisation of work, imbecility of culture, and so forth.[8]

What this analysis reveals, among other things, is that we should learn to resist the manner in which the capitalist market place attempts to lull us into a sense of false complacency by giving us the impression that it is objectively efficient. It will build universities, concert halls, art galleries, sports fields, and a host of other social amenities, but for what purpose? For sure, a soccer stadium is a good thing, but is it unimportant that today we associate South African soccer teams with products advertised on their jerseys as well as all over the stadium, rather than with the efficacy of physical culture? Sport has become money. Our traffic lights, therefore, no doubt a result of valuable science and technology, are a convenience which may also serve extremely complex ideological ends. But before we go further into this matter let us look at the kind of conspiracy that can exist between the corporate world and the seemingly elevating world of culture. We look at an example that comes from our own history.

Tim Couzens, in a significant piece of restorative work, reveals how way back in the 1920s and 1930s, film was used as a means of controlling labour in the mines. The book is called *The New African:*

A Study of the Life and Work of H.I.E. Dhlomo, and the relevant chapter is entitled 'Moralising Leisure Time (1882–1936)'. In this chapter, Couzens seeks to show how 'culture and entertainment can be used as an auxiliary force in social control'.[9] A group of white, liberal missionaries in the 1920s, faced with the large influx of Africans into the cities, the rise of slums and their attendant social problems, as well as the recent Land Act of 1914, sought to find ways of rescuing Africans from such a potentially corrupting social environment, while also stemming the tide of the potential political discontent that may rise to uncontrollable heights among Africans. They had two targets: 'the blacks who lived and worked in the city and mine labourers in the compounds'.[10] Attempts were to be made to educate these blacks through entertainment.

In the mines, film was going to be used for this purpose: 'We must capture the physical and mental life of these young men during six days of the week besides preaching the Gospel to them on the seventh', wrote Revd Ray Philips.[11] After volleyball and soccer had somewhat caught on, the magic of film did the job. Here is how Revd Ray Philips described the success of film:

> The result was immediate and gratifying. The thousands gathered around the screen and showed their appreciation by filling the compounds so full of joyful sound that outsiders often decided that a riot was occurring. With amazed delight the happy crowds went off on trips on the modern magic carpet to other lands; saw the surf riders of Honolulu, the explorers in the Arctic, the reindeer of Lapland and the potter's wheel in India. They followed with quaking breath the adventures of some of the early pioneers among the Indians in Western America; saw King George go to open Parliament in his curious equipage. But they shook their heads at pictures of mining in England and America, showing white men at work with pick and shovel and drill: 'Aikona! No, that is not right! Mfundisi is fooling us here! No white man works like that. Only black men!'[12]

No doubt, a picture of childlike, enthralled miners was proof of how easy it would be to keep them busy. It is possible that if further study was made on this subject, it might reveal that the apparent success of the programme of film shows in the mines led to a general government policy on the provision of entertainment to the rest of the African population throughout the country.

However, for the urban African, more sophisticated plans were afoot. Social centres were to be provided where the urban dweller would participate in activities such as reading, debates, indoor games, the production of plays, and ballroom dancing. Boy Scout and Girl Guide Movements would take care of the young. Thus concludes Couzens on the salutary effects of reading according to R.H.W. Shepherd:

> While there is no evidence for insincerity or hypocrisy on Shepherd's part, a distinct pattern of underlying assumptions emerges from his actions and writings. Clearly the activity of reading and the institution of libraries were important ways in which blacks could be accumulated into the 'new civilisation' whose value was scarcely doubted. The values of 'good literature' would thus be inculcated and the calm, dispassionate, sedentary nature of the activity would no doubt be salutary.[13]

What is of particular interest to us about these examples from the past is not so much the films themselves, or the other cultural activities as such, their value or lack of value would be the proper subject of another discussion. What should be of real interest to us today is the actual provision of physical facilities: film-showing arenas, mobile libraries, gramophones and records, and social centres such as the Bantu Men's Social Centre, the YMCA and the YWCA. Later we would have what came to be called Community Halls, Community Schools. Particular facilities were provided for the specific purpose of using cultural practice for social control. Underlying these institutions therefore, is a particular notion of art: art civilises natives by exposing them to western culture and thus reducing their capacity to resist that culture in its totality, and that totality includes its political and economic institutions and the laws governing their operations. Culture was designed to socialise the oppressed into accepting the foreign parameters of their domination. These facilities, therefore, were created for the purposes of acculturation.

It should not be difficult to appreciate why for the majority of the urban oppressed, particularly the petty bourgeoisie, it was the form of the medium of culture rather than the message that was the focus of interest, for the form was easily associated with advancement. Reading maketh a man. But what do you read? What is the context in which the reading takes place? And so, I suppose, does ballroom dancing also maketh a man. And so does going to the movies. It does not matter that you're going to see the Lone Ranger, Tarzan, and Donald Duck cartoons. The point is, being there, where a film is being shown is advancement. Consequently, there developed an imitative cultural behaviour generally lacking in content. It is this that became the 'official' culture of the townships.

All these 'cultural' activities would take place in what came to be called Community Halls or Community Schools, or buildings like the Bantu Men's Social Centre built for the purpose. The names of these buildings identify their designated ideological function. They indicate their origins in colonial anthropology to designate facilities for 'culturally backward people'. In this context then, these facilities performed the function of acculturation, and were not meant to provide occasions in which people would be able to reflect seriously on themselves and their environment. This situation has continued up until today.

Central to the quest for liberation in South Africa today is the quest for knowledge: the kind of knowledge that would lead to and be a significant contribution to the struggle for liberation. It is this knowledge that would enable the oppressed to speak with a new voice. Clearly, if what the oppressed masses of South Africa want to get back is their voice; if, as a result, everything at the moment is the need for content, for there is no doubt that the art of the moment is that form that offers most the promise of the advancement of knowledge and the deepening of insight (I'm thinking of all forms of art involving the word, whether articulated or written), then, as far as art is concerned, we have to refocus our understanding of its place in society. The example of literature may once more be helpful here.

Where before, reading was a mere function of social advancement; where it has been chiefly an indicator of acculturation; where it has been a functional activity to enable workers to read instructions and become better servants; where to read fiction has been to read industrially produced romance and superstition, then the more creative, liberating, and positive values of reading have to be restored. Reading has to be seen as the deepening of insight; as the broadening of intellectual horizons in the serious search for solutions to problems thrown up, in the first instance, by our immediate environment; as a vehicle of vital information about that environment; and, no less importantly, as the enjoyment of, as well as a reflection on, the miracle of human language. Politically, reading will be seen and regarded as an important extension of the democratic process itself. For reading is one of those social activities in the context of which ideas ought necessarily to be debated, and one which also contributes to the development of a critical social habit of thought.

The need then, in general, is that we entertain the notion of 'committed leisure' in which our attitude towards what are known presently as places of entertainment becomes a lot more serious. Theatres, according to this view, become places to which we go not because we want to show how cultured we are, but because we are going to explore with the actors issues that concern us deeply. Theatre then, becomes a place in which the issues addressed in lecture rooms, in centres of government are explored within the leisurely, though no less serious context of drama. It is in this sense that I say art should properly speaking be regarded as an extension of the democratic process. Only from that perspective can we really appreciate the fundamental social need for it.

The implications for this on the character of progressive political intervention in culture should already be evident. The political wing of the struggle, no doubt at the forefront of this struggle, should not make concessions to cultural practice. They should plan for it as a matter of necessity, for it is the only social context in which people are uninhibitedly themselves. For this reason, we should not 'include' culture as an after-thought in social planning. On the contrary, we should say, there can be no democratic society without the progressive institutionalisation of cultural practice, *in all its forms*.

The matter can be restated differently. The arts should not be regarded as a mere means to an end – as a means to manipulate public thought, for example. That is one function they can play. But that function can degenerate into being a purely manipulative venture in which even those in the forefront of the struggle can use art to limit and contain the expressive capacity of the people. For that reason, the manipulative function of art can be a potentially reactionary one. The need is consciously to accord the arts a structural function in society. The justification for this need should derive from the nature of the society we envisage rather than from a limited political programme. The function of art in society should outlive the limits of a specific political programme of action. In other words, instead of asserting that we need the arts to mobilise people, as a primary goal, rather, we should say we need the arts because they extend the limits of democratic participation. So it should be with cultural practice in general.

At issue is a rigorous critique of existing cultural practice and institutions and a determined groping towards fundamental and liberating alternatives. We aim not only at changing the content of our cultural expression, but also at efficient social organisation where such expression can be assigned a definite place. The aim is to restore to the community of the oppressed, a practical sense of organised and organic civic society. This, I believe, could be done through a concerted focus on the actual material dimensions of civic society. For the oppressed do have a culture; what they need to do is pay closer attention to its material expression during the process of struggle, such that that culture itself can constitute the material content of a changing alternative consciousness.

We are going to be heirs to a highly complex industrial and technological culture which may even include a nuclear arsenal. What an awesome responsibility! The aim is not to allow ourselves to be overwhelmed by this culture and the rigidly entrenched methods of its operation which have become second nature to those whose behaviour has been completely conditioned through this culture of oppression; rather, it is to understand it, throwing away all its evils, while making its best aspects available to the enrichment of the emergent and highly creative alternative culture. That, would be the nature of our contribution to the universal struggle for liberty.

NOTES

1. Peter Horn, 'A Preparatory Note on Peter Weiss, His Novel. *The Aesthetics of Resistance and its Relevance to the South African Situation*', *Critical Arts*, Vol.3, No.4, p.1.
2. Ariel Dorfman, *The Empire's Old Clothes*, (New York: Pantheon Books, 1983), p.3.
3. Ariel Dorfman, p.5.
4. Ariel Dorfman, p.5.
5. Miroslav Marek, Milan Hromadka, Josef Chroust, *Cultural Policy in Czechoslovakia*, (Paris: UNESCO, 1970), p.15.
6. Amilcar Cabral, *Unity and Struggle*, (London: Heinemann AWS, 1980), pp.139–40.
7. Kwame Nkrumah, *Consciencism: Philosophy and Ideology for De-Colonisation*, (London: Panaf, 1964), p.63.
8. Joel Kovel, *The Age of Desire*, (New York: Pantheon Books, 1981), pp.170–1.
9. Tim Couzens, *The New African: A Study of the Life and Work of H.I.E. Dhlomo*, (Johannesburg: Ravan Press, 1985), p.92.
10. Tim Couzens, p.93.
11. Tim Couzens, p.96.
12. Tim Couzens, p.96.
13. Tim Couzens, p.106.

7

❖ ❖ ❖

AGAINST PAMPHLETEERING
THE FUTURE

From the theme of this conference, 'South Africa: Beyond the Platitudes', it could be suggested that there are at least two ways by which ruling authorities can exert control over people. The first way involves the creation of a climate of political debate in which people are made to feel that they are at the cross-roads of history, and that difficult and fundamental decisions have to be made and serious sacrifices demanded of everyone. A series of principles are set forth as determining the shape of the future. It is on such principles that the nature of government may have to be altered, and new opportunities for the governed created in the fields of education, industry, commerce, agriculture, and general social welfare. Ultimately, to facilitate the birth of the envisaged kingdom, even the way people think and behave will accordingly have to be altered drastically. A new, ideal person will have to be brought into being according to the requirements of the future. In other words, everyone must be made to feel that there is a formidable mission to be undertaken.

It can reasonably be asserted that for the white people of South Africa, the period between 1910 and 1948 may be regarded as a formative one in which were established the major determinants of

This essay was presented as the keynote address at the inaugural conference of the Congress of South African Writers, Johannesburg, July, 1987.

a white kingdom of power and prosperity. However flawed the debate, it would be hard to deny that from the point of view of the white electorate, this period was essentially constructive. It was constructive not in an ethical sense, but in the sense that a defined political direction consolidated itself into a powerful national movement setting a dominant pattern of social behaviour for all of us.

After a relatively long passage of time, in our case forty years of Nationalist rule, we witness an historical transition to the second way of social control. For the vast majority of whites the predominant social reality of apartheid was no longer something to be actively argued for or justified on moral, political, social, religious, or other grounds. It was a given universal reality that has been there and would always be there to the end of time. The serious issues of national construction, of defining a vision (no matter how flawed the vision) and the human attributes necessary to achieving that vision are no longer there. Instead, intellectual activity in general has shifted away from a concern with original principles, to a concern with the maintenance and consolidation of a political and material culture that is a legacy of forty years of dominance. Consequently, under the social habit of domination, the general political and intellectual culture of white South Africa has suffered a gradual decadence as it slowly shed its constitutive features in order to assume a purely manipulative character.

But the relative absence of a redemptive intellectual culture does not mean the absence of intelligence. It simply spells the social trivialisation of the collective intellect. We have now entered the age of platitudes in which the search is no longer for ultimate solutions, but for convenient adjustments. Indeed, it is the age of ad hoc councils, various advisory bodies, consulting agencies, commissions of all kinds, research institutes, marketing surveys, and opinion polls of all shades. All these take advantage of an academic culture that has been turned into a commodity after having been subdued by a technological approach to society. Thriving on the euphoria of the political and economic success of the last four decades, this age responds to the needs of both the whites and the oppressed by striving to suggest that all is well; that any problem can be efficiently taken care of.

To the whites, the age encapsulates them in a cloud of comforting benevolence towards the oppressed. It says to them: 'we are in charge; here to stay. But we must find a *formula* for letting them in. Our lifestyle is the supreme international standard. They are lucky to have us here. Let us educate them. Let us guide them carefully through the intricacies of our thought, our institutions, our customs. We are the way to their salvation. Let us turn them into ourselves. That way, we can ensure the continuation of our usual lifestyle. Some minor adjustments will have to be made but nothing will really change. You'll be taken care of. Look around you at the glaring evidence of our achievements!'

The age then turns to the oppressed and says: 'look at all the evidence of the white man's achievement around you. You really didn't have to spend agonising moments thinking and planning all this. You were spared the difficult tasks. Yet, now, these wonderful things are yours to enjoy. You, the most fortunate among oppressed peoples. The most honoured. Take it all: the ninety-nine-year lease, so that you can build any kind of house you like; every cinema and restaurant is available for your entertainment; register your children in a white private school; rise to the highest managerial levels of any company. The sky is the limit. The freedom of this land is yours only if you concentrate on enjoying its wealth and its institutions. In all these things, the rules, regulations, laws, social customs, and a host of procedures have been set in place for you. They have been carefully thought out and set in place over the years. Don't worry. Don't worry about governing the land. Don't even think about it. It's too daunting a task. Okay, we'll give you some local authority and 'own affairs' business. But in general, government is in good hands. Just follow the rules and regulations. Just be good and all will be well. Okay? All the best!'

Behind all this, as we can see, is a manipulative intelligence which despises the intelligence of the entire population at the same time as

143

it proclaims their humanity. That, is the measure of its decadence. It calls for the infantilisation of the oppressed by asking them to be civilised oppressed people. The chief mark of the civilised oppressed person is that he can see 'civilisation' without seeing the oppression. He is one whose critical consciousness has been lulled by promise of material gratification.

I am now going to spend some time looking at some of the mechanisms of modern South African oppression. I use the word 'modern' to underscore the fact that the techniques of oppression have evolved over the years, assuming greater refinement in line with the increasing technical competence of South African capitalism. In doing so, though, I'll be addressing myself specifically to the uses of the written word in so far as it is used to create the impression of a social order so appealing and comforting that the resulting illusion can blunt the legitimacy of the struggle, thus severely compromising it. I am going to use, as a context of discussion and analysis, a recent phenomenon that has occurred in Duduza.

Ever since the people of Duduza rose up against the terrible conditions of life to which they had been so insensitively subjected over the years, they have witnessed a strange, relatively new phenomenon: the planting of pamphlets. They grow fast, these pamphlets, like mushrooms. Suddenly they'll be there in the morning, when they were not there before people went to bed the previous night. Or they will be found at home in the evening when people return from work. They'll be there, waiting to be picked up freely and read, promising the revelation of truth and the coming of redemption. Certainly, some 'mysterious force' has suddenly acknowledged that indeed, the people of Duduza are people. They definitely can read; that they too are capable of deriving some benefits from the civilising activity of reading. Here is an unedited example of one of the original pamphlets mysteriously bequeathed to the people of Duduza as a gift of the night:

Each one reach one — for peace
WHO ARE THE STOOGES OF RUSSIA

144

IT IS THE ANC, THE UDF AND CIVIC ASSOCIATION

What did these comrades reach through their struggle. They caused the death of your brothers and sisters, children and innocent people. They caused the los of peoples homes through arson, the disruption of schools so that your children will remain uneducated WHILE THEIR CHILDREN ARE SAVE IN PRIVATE SCHOOLS OR EVEN OVERSEAS TO GET EDUCATION. They caused the bus boicot which has let your fathers and mothers to walk and suffer unnecessary.

They cause the consumer boicot to destroy and confiscate you and your childrens hard earned food. Thus they prevent you the freedom they shout about so loudly.

THESE SO CALLED FREEDOM FIGHTERS ARE THE PUPPETS AND STOOGES OF RUSSIA. They even use your churches to meet instead of to worship God and to live a life of love as God teach us to do. Love your fellowmen. Love that do not put a necklace around you brothers neck. Love that we respect and honour each other and that will bring happiness.

WHY IS THERE PEACE AND NO TROUBLE WHILE THE SELF APPOINTED SO CALLED LEADERS AND PUPPETS OF RUSSIA ARE IN JAIL BECAUSE THEY ONLY WANT DESTRUCTION, CHAOS, DEATH STARVATION AND HATRED

WE DO NOT WANT PEOPLES COURTS WE DO NOT WANT TO BE RULED AND LASHED BY CHILDREN WE WANT TO MAKE USE OF THE BUSSERVICE

We do not want our groceries destroyed by children

Let us join hands, let us join forces, let us stop fithing and let us build Duduza again.

Let us be quiet and think. Think what damages was done.

Think what we are to do from now and into the future to improve our township, our lives, our homes, schools and families.

Let us not teach one to destroy but rather let EACH ONE REACH ONE FOR PEACE Down with struggle, rather communicate and co-operate in order to get progress in out township.

Let us work together

Let us pray together

Let us stay together

DUDUZA PEACE MOVEMENT

The effect of this pamphlet depends less on what it says than on what it leaves unsaid. Behind the direct attack on identified targets, the 'stooges of Russia', is the assumption that there is something of value that has been threatened. The pamphlet suggests that there is a community of interest that exists and has always existed in Duduza. This community of interest also implies a strong sense of collective responsibility on the part of each and every resident of Duduza. The pamphlet then conjures before the people a seemingly unmistakable common sense of purpose, one that has always brought the people of Duduza together. It says that Duduza has always been a secure, well ordered community, centred around the family, the church, the school, the community hall, shops, and the administration offices. Consequently, the people of Duduza have always happily boarded their busses to go to work; have always returned from work to enjoy a happy drink at the beer hall; have always done their shopping without problems; have worshipped with grace and sincerity, without any interference; have loved one another as fellowmen. Order, peace, love, and plenty have reigned supreme in Duduza for as long as anyone can remember. Until the coming of 'the stooges of Russia'! Even more wonderful, this perfect state of social being appears to have been achieved without any kind of strife, struggle, and sacrifice. The people of Duduza have always forged ahead effortlessly, and everything just worked out: until the coming of 'the stooges of Russia'! All these truths are self-evident: that since there has never been crime in Duduza; since there has never been a single incident of police harassment; since there has never been any alcoholism; since there have never been crowded, ill-equipped, understaffed schools; since there has never been a time when there was no sewerage system, or water in every house; since there has always been street lighting; and, yes, since there has never been a single instance of embezzlement of church funds, Duduza has no history of discontent. Therefore, there is absolutely no reason for any kind of discontent. Discontent is an irrational expression of ingratitude; and ingratitude must be stamped out resolutely. People of Duduza, 'let each one reach one for peace'.

But why does the pamphlet adopt an inherently disingenuous position. Why does it display no sense of irony whatsoever? Firstly, the writers of the pamphlet may actually believe in the illusion. Their collaboration with the status quo may have resulted in a package of personal benefits for them such that their capacity to differentiate between truth and falsehood became distorted. They have so internalised the image of the oppressor that they have become indistinguishable from him. Secondly, the pamphlet may have well been produced by people who were fully aware of the vast resources of the science of deception. These are masters in the manipulation of human perceptions. These are the creative inventors of platitudes. One thing they have depended upon in this pamphlet, something of direct interest to this gathering, is the complex history of the written word, a history which they have thrown with great vigour at people who, by and large, have been deprived of the opportunity to understand that history. They know that there will be many people in Duduza who will look at the pamphlet and doubt the evidence of their own experience. They know that these people, like the bewildered animals in *Animal Farm*, will look at the indisputable evidence of the written word, and agree that indeed, other animals have always been more equal. It has always been so.

People can be affected this way by writing because writing is essentially a subversive act. It has the powerful capability to invade in a very intimate manner, the personal world of the reader. Whenever you read, you risk being affected in a manner that can change the course of your life. This power of subversion lies in the seemingly infallible testimony of the written word. Consequently, its authority is potentially tyrannical. But then, the source of this authority has a long history. It is a history that has surrounded the written word with awe, persuading us that what is written necessarily contains unalterable, profound wisdom. The priests of Ancient Egypt long effectively established this awesome power when they prevented commoners from ever getting near the written word. This imbued it with magic, with the result that the written word loomed large in the imagination of the larger population as something mysteriously powerful, delivering unalterable judgements. Later, there followed religious texts of all sorts such as the Bible, the Koran and others which became texts containing ultimate and unquestionable wisdom. And so down the path of history, government proclamations, and a host of 'official documents' became repositories of uncontested truth. Indeed, where lies the authority of the school, the university? Certainly, and in large measure, in the presence there of textbooks, of the library, of written rules and regulations, and of the authenticated certificates of teachers. The certificate on the wall! There it is, on special paper, decorated, signed and framed as the ultimate witness to an uncontested truth.

And so, in Duduza, the declamatory pamphlet soon gives way to something more permanent. It was followed by a newsletter. In the context of social strife, a context tactically denied by the system, a newsletter works on the assumption that tremendous events are taking place and people need to be informed. It assumes an admirable democratic public spiritedness on the part of the producer of the newsletter. So, taking advantage of the fact that finally, a sewerage system was going to be introduced in Duduza, the Duduza administration released what was first called *Duduza Press*, subtitled 'A Newsletter that tells you Everything that is Happening in your Township'. However, after a competition obviously meant to advertise the newsletter as well as to create public identification with it, the newsletter was renamed *Duduzani*, and here is how the results of the competition were announced:

> The competition announced in the previous edition to choose
> a suitable name for the newsletter, was won by Florence

Sepenyane of 2170 Nala Street, Duduza. She suggested we call the newsletter 'DUDUZANI', and won herself R50,00. Congratulations Florence, you can collect your prize money from Mrs. Henning at the administration offices.

The character of this issue of *Duduzani* can be gleaned from the headlines on the various reports: 'News Received from the Apex Training Centre', 'Urgent Notice to Parents', 'Holiday Programme', 'FREE Video Shows', 'Christmas Greetings', 'Competition Time Again', 'A Note from the CIRCUIT INSPECTOR', 'GOOD NEWS for our Senior Citizens', 'SADF vs Local Teachers', 'Reunion: Hiking Trip', 'Chess', 'Soccer', 'Sports Course: Zandspruit', and 'Boxing'. The total picture presented is one of absolutely calm, peaceful and normal society. Moreover, it has always been like this. There is no conflict in Duduza, and there never has been any, really. If there is any conflict at all, it is of the friendly kind in the context of organised sports: what with the SADF playing soccer and chess against Duduza residents! The confusing ambiguity this kind of thing causes in people unsure of themselves, people who have not built up defenses against this kind of onslaught, may very well result in their grudging agreement that indeed, there have always been animals more equal than others. What we have is the quintessential, manipulative politics of platitudes.

This publication, *Duduzani*, coming in the wake of the long delayed improvement of the physical infrastructure in Duduza, brings up before us another kind of text, perhaps more menacing under the circumstances. The infrastructure represents another kind of pamphlet: it is the high-rise office buildings, houses of parliament, the complex network of roads, railways, and airports, military academies, white universities, private schools, hospitals, research institutes, chambers of commerce, banks, factories, hotels, opera houses, sports arenas, in other words, all the visible symbols of capitalist achievement, all of which the oppressed would like to claim. All these, as shown above, are suddenly available to the oppressed, there for the taking, provided they agree to be law abiding, civilised oppressed people.

With the sewerage, the newly tarred streets, new schools, the people of Duduza are well on their way. Clearly the activity of reading is not confined only to deciphering the written word, reading also takes place as we walk around absorbing the language of architecture, and being affected by the various uses to which the art of building has been put to suggest the power of orderly society.

Looked at from a necessary historical perspective, if only to show how little the essential mechanisms of domination have changed, we need to make the intriguing observation that the mirrors of old, together with those intoxicating bottles of whiskey, presented by European settlers to fascinated Africans, in exchange for cattle and vast tracts of land, are still as fascinating as ever. The main difference, of course, is that today not only have we had a hand in their making, but also that this time, it will not be land and cattle we will be giving away, but something infinitely more valuable: our very humanity, acquired through our engineered compliance. And so, in this way, the attraction of 'civilisation' is rendered more powerful in comparison to the need to revolt on behalf of something new and untested. Indeed, the pervasive power of technical efficiency, extended to an array of government institutions, commerce, and industry can create the overwhelming impression that it is far better to be absorbed and conform, and utterly useless to resist. The culture of technical efficiency aims at creating a sense of social well-being which depends on the instant satisfaction of needs. To be caught, it is necessary to be placed firmly in the cycle of need and instant gratification.

What are the implications of all this on South African writing? The power of the written word in the moulding of social perceptions should never be taken for granted. The professional manufacturers of artificial social needs for commodities have never taken this wisdom for granted. Nor have they taken for granted the power of the surrounding reality as it presents itself to us as a vast social text sending complex, often competing messages. These texts complement each other closely. This close relationship suggests that the business of writing and that of defining and then transforming the world are more intimately related than is usually granted. Both texts are a visible manifestation of the history of social thought as well as the history of the practical satisfaction of human needs. For this reason, therefore, the oppressed of South Africa will want to re-enter the contest for power in history with both their minds and their hands. They will accept no assurances that the thinking and the doing have been done for them. They will want nothing less than the writing of their own texts.

The path towards the new text should begin with the understanding that it is precisely where the official culture of South African oppression runs aground and becomes decadent and manipulative that the oppressed must come up with a reconstitutive political and intellectual culture that will recreate and re-energise civilisation in this country. In practical terms it means that a manipulative culture must be confronted squarely through a consistent exposure of its emptiness, as well as through a radical substitution of that emptiness with reconstructive content. As far as the latter is concerned in particular, the oppressed will need to say: 'we have thoughts we want to validate through the written word so that we too can participate in the historical contest of texts for authority. In practical terms, our writings will be filled with answers to the following questions, among many others: what is the real function of all these buildings? What is the meaning of the home for the aged? The designs of these cities, what needs are they intended to meet? What is the real purpose of all these laws? Why should we drive on the left of the road? Why should we have only two official languages? Why should we vote at the end of every four years? Why doesn't the airline menu include our favourite dishes? Why should we fill in this form that demands the colour of our skins? What is the aim of all this research? Why should there be nuclear weapons? Why are we not there in all the things that really matter? Why is the "Great Trek" not the Calamitous Invasion?' There are thousands of texts to be written. The oppressor, who has deliberately left millions of people outside of all serious human activity, will definitely have to learn to live with the fact that there are going to be drastic revisions to his own texts.

In general, it means that since our interest is in fundamental issues, since we want to recreate the entire social order, we must avoid the way of the manipulative pamphlet. We must not pamphleteer the future. Nor should we pamphleteer the past. To pamphleteer the future is to reduce complex issues to simple formulations such that understanding is prevented, or at best, clouded. Pamphleteering the future means writing that establishes its case without the onus of proof; writing that challenges without educating, that is heroic without being too convinced of its heroism. Pamphleteering the future might also mean conviction without knowledge. It is writing that is not conscious of the extent to which it may have internalised the textual strategies of the oppressor. Specifically, it means that the common aim of all writers, at this point in our history, is to assail relentlessly the textual authority of oppression and replace it with the textual authority of liberation; and that the essential characteristics of the new text are its seriousness, its radical broad-mindedness, its inventiveness, its unbounded respect for the reader, and its understanding that no aspect of the life of the oppressed is irrelevant as a subject for artistic or expository treatment.

What are the practical implications of these observations? We need to realise, for a start, that, although this conference has brought together practitioners of a certain kind of writing, there are other kinds of writing that are equally important. In fact, I would submit that creative writing will not grow very much with the simultaneous flourishing of the writings of ideas, of fact and information giving, of genuine polemical debate. We need to create a broad literary culture founded on the understanding that writing in all its various forms represents the attempt of the human mind to reach out towards ever increasing intellectual refinement. It represents an attempt at disciplined reflection. Consequently, we want to aim for a future inhabited by highly informed people. To move towards that society, we want to insist that as many opportunities as possible should be created for people to write, read and to study the word, to understand both its strengths and its limitations. The aim of our writing should be to break the potentially repressive tyranny of the written word by emphasising the fact that texts are to be questioned and debated with. Here the power of creative writing is particularly relevant, for only there is language freed from association with a purely manipulative function. The truth of literature is to be found in its power to allow readers to formulate insights independently of outside authority. To allow them to recreate themselves by enabling them to freely write their own texts.

It may be wondered why I have put so much emphasis on the written word. What about oral literature? The central belief behind my emphasis is that the written word is an inescapable fact of modern life. This is not to deny the importance of oral literature but merely to assert the fact that the relatively greater impact of the written word in the social contest for power is undeniable. To assert the contrary is to dangerously romanticise the oral tradition. It is to deny the mass reader the opportunity to experience the efficacy of self-education through reading. The aim is to enable the ordinary reader to domesticate the written word for his own liberation.

The people of Duduza have continued to press forward with their demands. They tell us that they have not bought the lie. But they do need the assurance of written testimony that theirs is the way of truth. What are the elements of this truth? The search for those elements and their definition through discussion and debate is what should replace the dead age of platitudes. One of the central challenges of this conference is to find ways of how to go about initiating the newness through the contribution of the art of the word.

8

❖ ❖ ❖

THE WRITERS' MOVEMENT
IN SOUTH AFRICA

Some forty years ago, in July 1947, Jordan Ngubane, the editor of
Inkundla ya Bantu placed 'an idea before the nation's thinkers' in
the form of a suggestion that an African Academy of Arts be
established. Anton Lembede, the first president of the Youth League
of the African National Congress, welcomed the idea, adding that
'we need African Artists to interpret the spirit of Africa'.[1]

But credit for a more detailed expression of support for Jordan
Ngubane's call must go to A.P. Mda, an active and articulate member
of the Youth League. Not only did Mda embrace the idea, he also
gave substance to it by suggesting its form and functions. The
Academy, he said should be a All-African affair. Any attempt to
make it heterogeneous is bound to break down on the hard rock of
reality. It should not even be a non-European affair. Whilst we should
co-operate with other non-Europeans and even Europeans, to
advance the general course of art, we should however have our purely
African Academy to advance the peculiar and particular needs of
African Art.

Secondly, the Academy should not be tribalist in orientation. Its
purpose should broadly embrace all sections of the African
population in the Union and the Protectorates.

'Thirdly, the method of organisation of such a venture should
depend on the peculiar circumstances of the artists in each area. No

hard and fast method can be decided upon beforehand. What obviously there would be need for to begin with is an organising committee whose task would be to tap all available sources in preparation for an all-in congress of African artists summoned to a centrally situated venue like Bloemfontein. This would at once create an executive to frame a constitution and regulations'.[2]

This attempt at starting a relevant cultural organisation was not an isolated one. Two years later, in 1949, members of the Youth League at Fort Hare wrote a letter to the press 'pleading' according to Tim Couzens, for the creation of an African Academy. They claimed that up to that time African sculpture and painting had been looked upon as 'mere curiosities' and they suggested that no proper interpretation of the spirit of the artist had been made. They went on to suggest that music and literary manuscripts should also be collected: 'Nothing that breathes the spirit of Africa should be left out'. A monthly magazine should also be produced. Finally, they suggested that the Academy (comprising an art gallery, museum, repository for literary works, newscuttings section, music section) be located at Fort Hare.[3]

September 1948 saw yet another attempt. H.I.E. Dhlomo tried to organise a Society of African Authors, Artists and Musicians. This attempt did not succeed.[4]

Many decades later, South African writers are still trying to establish writers' organisations with the same passion with which their forebearers attempted to do so. For example, the last ten years in South Africa have witnessed intense efforts at organising writers. There were six major waves. In 1974 the Writers' and Artists' Guild of South Africa was established. Then there was the phenomenal mushrooming of writers and cultural groups of all kinds in the townships throughout the country in the mid-seventies. There were at least twenty-five recorded ones. PEN (Johannesburg) followed in 1978, and when it disbanded in 1982, it was immediately replaced by the African Writers' Association which still exists. In 1985 the Writers' Forum was created, but in July 1987, it became the Congress of South African Writers, which still exists. A brief profile of each organisation will be helpful.

The Guild was basically an organisation of white writers which, according to Lionel Abrahams, 'would have welcomed black artists to its ranks but for some reason black applicants were not forthcoming and its membership remained white'.[5] It further described itself as 'a non-racial group that seeks to protect the interests of writers and artists against the interference of the State or censorship'. Beyond that the Guild also sought to promote new work, and to circulate information by means of a quarterly newsletter, as well as to hold frequent readings.[6]

The emergence of numerous cultural groups in the townships in the mid-seventies was, without doubt, a singular event in the contemporary cultural history of South Africa. They came in various names and from various parts of the country: Creative Youth Association of Diepkloof, Soweto; Moakeng League of Painters and Authors (MALEPA) of Bloemfontein and Kroonstad; Ga-Rankuwa Art Association; the Guyo Book Club of Sibasa; Mpumalanga Arts of Hammarsdale; Community Arts Project of Cape Town; Peyarta (Port Elizabeth Young Artists' Association), and several others.

This phenomenon was a product of the climate of resistance that owed much of its character and thrust to the Black Consciousness Movement. In this connection, for example, it has been noted that the two prominent motifs in *Staffrider* are those of 'blackness and revolt'.[7] Their distinguishing characteristic was advocacy of the performing arts. A group such as the Medupe was an outstanding example of this tendency. Poetry was recited to the beat of drums. Otherwise there was much drama and music. Some of the first performances of such well known plays as Matsemela Manaka's *Egoli* took place in the context of group cultural activities. The declared intention often was to resuscitate the African oral tradition; to stress the traditional functionality of art now enlisted for the purposes of political mobilisation.

Written literature was provided with a very useful avenue in *Staffrider* magazine which took advantage of the publishing capacity of Ravan Press. The magazine wanted to encourage this flowering of artistic activity by leaving editorial decisions to contributing art groups. Its editorial policy was articulated as follows: To be published in *Staffrider* is to be read – more widely, we reckon, than literary artists have ever been read in South Africa.

> We define a literary artist simply: a producer of literary works. And we believe that a producer has a basic right of access to potential readers – in the immediate community in which he or she lives and beyond.
>
> The phenomenon of art groups linked to particular township communities in present-day South Africa suggests the appropriate medium through which this basic right can be exercised. The art group puts forward the work it wants to be published, and then assists in the distribution of the magazine to the community. In this way editorial control is vested in the writers as participants in a community-based group.
>
> Those who suggest that *Staffrider* should appoint an editor whose task is to impose 'standards' on the magazine are expressing – consciously or unconsciously – an elitist view of art which cannot comprehend the new artistic energies released in the tumult of 1976 and after. Standards are not golden or quintessential: they are made according to the demands different societies make on writers, and according to the responses writers make to those demands.
>
> If standards are not imposed by elitist criticism but developed and maintained by practicing writers the 'workshop' concept becomes crucial. It is here, in effect, that standards are set. We do not know of a writers' group that would not welcome participation of critics in its workshop sessions: this is an invitation to leave the armchair or the lectern and become involved, practically, in building a new literature.[8]

In each issue of *Staffrider* much space was devoted to group contributions. But suddenly, after the third number of Volume 3, in 1980, *Staffrider* stopped bringing out group contributions. The era of township cultural groups seemed over after a brief and invigorating time.

The following is an example of a typical group. It was introduced to the public in an early issue of *Staffrider* in the following manner:

> The name MADI is derived from the acronym made from the first letters in music, arts and drama, and the 'i' is taken from literature. This is, in short, what this Katlehong-based group is all about.
>
> In its infancy the group has already brought together a number of up and coming Katlehong artists, poets, writers and dramatists.
>
> Top of the group's regular activities is the Madi Arts Fair. The first of these monthly fairs was in January where CYA's musical group, Babupi, were the central attraction, and an extract from Matsemela Manaka's play, *Egoli*, was performed.
>
> A weekly Arts Academy for the serious study of the arts, conducted by invited experts, is run by the group at the Katlehong Art Centre in Phooko Section.
>
> Madi is destined to be a milestone in the appreciation of the arts in Katlehong. Madi writers who have appeared in previous issued of *Staffrider* are Letshaba Thubela and Moloto wa Moloto.[9]

PEN (Johannesburg) came about in 1978 as a daring effort to bring together members of the Guild and the Township groups. *Staffrider* did much through its pages to promote this movement. Naturally, bringing together organisations with memberships of such different social, class and political backgrounds would create special difficulties. For example, there was much disagreement over questions of membership. Some members wanted to confine memberships to published writers only. While others wanted the attribute 'writer' to be extended to journalists. There was also much debate over the kind of workshops PEN would organise. Should they be practical workshops grappling with artistic form, or should they be discussions on content, covering such topics as relevant artistic themes, the role of art in society, the responsibilities of writers, etc.? Should readings be by invitation or should anyone just come and read and anyone was free to attend? The second alternative in each case won, giving rise to Lionel Abrahams observing that 'the shape, size and colour of PEN was being radically altered and its activities were going to be largely governed by its intimate connection with the township groups'.[10]

A typical and exciting example of the kind of activities PEN engaged in was reported in the April/May 1979 issue of *Staffrider*:

> Recently a 'writers' wagon' (two combis in fact) visited writers in the Cape. In the wagon there were representatives from various groups, Mpumalanga Arts Group (Hammarsdale), Malopoets (Mariannridge), Zamani Arts Association (Dobson-ville), Creative Youth Association (Diepkloof), Khauleza Creative Society (Alexandra), Madi Arts Group (Katlehong) and many more individual writers. The trip was made possible by the kind assistance of the British and Dutch people, through their local embassies. Soon another 'writers' wagon' will visit groups and writers in the North. All writers are invited to travel with PEN.[11]

Political pressures were meanwhile building up on the organisations. Many black writers began to find problematic the fact of being in the same organisation with white people. As the pressures mounted, PEN (Johannesburg) was forced to disband early in 1982.[12]

The African Writers' Association (AWA) became the home of those black writers who were dissatisfied with the white membership of PEN (Johannesburg). There was some debate about whether the organisation should be called the Black Writers' Association or the African Writers' Association. The latter name won as it was felt that the term 'black' did not carry any cultural connotation. Besides, only the Afrikaners, most ironically, would otherwise remain the only people called Africans in South Africa. Thus, AWA revealed its Black Consciousness orientation.

Basically, AWA attempted to inherit the cultural experience of the township groups, either to build on it or to resuscitate it. Its singular achievement has been the establishment of Skotaville. Otherwise, AWA attempted to establish branches throughout the country and to hold workshops for its members.

Meanwhile, writers were clearly feeling the pressure of increasingly polarised political developments in South Africa. Some writers were feeling that writers should be able to meet across the broad spectrum of political affiliation to discuss the problems of writers. The Writers' Forum was not intended to be a 'formal structured organisation', rather it was 'intended to be exactly what the word Forum intimates, i.e. a place where public discussion can be held. Without restriction, or fear of offending another's political probity'.[13] When the Forum met for the first time in July 1985, the African Writers' Association was not officially represented and did not participate in Forum activities.

At the second conference of the Writers' Forum in 1987, it was decided that writers could not just come together and talk shop, they had to do so from a clearly defined political position. The emerging view was that writers could not stand aloof from the massive political movements throughout the country embodied in the United Democratic Front, and the Congress of South African Trade Unions. Thus, the Congress of South African Writers was formed. The writers present there pledged themselves to devote their total creative resources to advance the struggle for the creation of a non-racial and democratic South Africa. Furthermore, they recognised that writers and cultural workers generally, are products of and belong to the community. As such, they have a responsibility to serve the community.

A common thread runs through the history of writers' and artists' organisations in South Africa: it is the history of either outright failure to establish such organisations or, where they were established, of their tragic transience.

The question would then have to be asked: why have writers' organisations generally failed to survive? Are they an inherently transient phenomenon? Or are there some identifiable objective reasons that are responsible for this transience? Asking such questions is particularly germane at this point in the development of the South African struggle for liberation. Existing organisations certainly need to draw on the experience of their predecessors. To this end, their efforts would need to be guided by an organised body of knowledge resulting from purposefully analysed past experience. Writers and cultural organisations, aiming at a certain degree of active permanence and constructive influence, need to benefit from the scientific approach towards organisational behaviour such as is brought to bear on other kinds of organisations: political and trade union organisations, for example. I'm not aware that this particular exercise has been seriously attempted before in South Africa. Hence, the thrust of my present effort will be speculative in an explorative and suggestive manner.

If we return to the early effort to establish the African Academy of Arts in the 1940s, we will note three crucial aspects to Mda's suggestion. Firstly, are the aims of the Academy 'to advance the peculiar and particular needs of African Art'; secondly is its membership which 'should be an All-African affair', and lastly, its 'method of organisation' which 'should depend on the peculiar circumstances of the artists in each area'. Following this example, these three aspects of organisational structuring have traditionally featured prominently in the formation of writers' organisations.

Unfortunately, Mda does not go on to specify exactly what the 'peculiar and particular needs of African Art' were, nor did he go on to give examples of what the 'peculiar circumstances of the artists in each area' were. The suggested 'Congress of African Artists' would most probably have discussed such issues in detail. Unfortunately, that important congress never took place. However, one thing, which is clearly implied in Mda's proposal, did not need a congress to articulate. It is the context of political objectives for which the African Academy of Arts was to be one practical manifestation among others. Central to these objectives was the overriding aim of creating a sense of common nationhood among the different African peoples of South Africa: what Lembede called, 'the creation of a homogeneous nation out of heterogeneous tribes'.[14] Thus, the projected membership of the Academy emerges as a crucial factor in its political identity.

It would be expected, of course, that the issue of membership of any organisation in South Africa should dominate discussion. The spectre of racism looms very large in the social consciousness. Consequently, there has tended to be, in general, a ready agreement in two areas: the aims of organisations and the organisational methods of pursuing those aims. For example, it is apparently not a contentious issue simply to declare that the organisation is meant 'to advance the peculiar and particular needs of African Art'. Indeed, it seems self-evident. So is it easy to declare that branches will have to be created throughout the country. Consequently, those areas of organisational life that would ensure the actual survival of the organisation as a visible and successful entity did not benefit from sustained critical scrutiny and debate. Thus, the articulation of aims and means essentially served the needs of mobilisation.

In this situation, what gives an organisation its legitimacy is its membership, because the question of membership, once resolved, situates the organisation within an identifiable political perspective in the political spectrum. This political perspective, embodied in the membership, rather than in clearly defined programmes of action, tends to take a sustained precedence over programmes of action which could practically sustain and validate political objectives. In the long run, assuming that political objectives have been identified, organ- isational efficiency is crucial to the success of the organisation. A brief example will suffice.

The Writers' and Artists' Guild was essentially a white organisa- tion which, however, was also keen to project its non-racial beliefs. PEN (Johannesburg), a non-racial organisation, broke up over the question of the racial composition of its membership. When the Writers' Forum was established, the debate in the press over member- ship questions was quite acrimonious. Still, it was pointed out by some of the debaters how the issue over membership actually clouded other substantive issues that were discussed at the first conference of the Forum.

Ironically, there may have been, in all cases, no fundamental disagreement over the aims of the organisations. Indeed, there was broad agreement on such issues as the need to combat all forms of censorship, to hold readings and workshops. Very conventional activities! Was all the fury justified only so that readings and workshops could follow? The concept of the writers' organisation, therefore, does not appear to have advanced beyond the political significance of the concept of membership. They have existed to prove the symbolic, political significance of their membership rather than to stress and explore further the efficacy of their activities. A crucial matter of emphasis.

In the midst of all this, another remarkable irony may be that the popular township groups were more successful as organisations precisely because they did not need to justify the racial composition of their membership. Black Consciousness in the townships had become an ethos rather than something to prove. It enjoyed the status of uncontested popularity. This situation is instructive. It suggests that writers' organisations are more likely to succeed where a political and cultural environment that can sustain them is strong.

The last observation is particularly important because it hints at the possibility of a certain kind of material vulnerability of such organisations. Writers' organisations, by definition, are not orientated towards material production. Because they are essentially a non-productive entity, clarity on their structural function in society is particularly vital. They are started essentially to provide a context for organised intellectual interventions within a specific kind of political environment. In South Africa that environment is currently the mass-based democratic movement and its concerted search for alternatives. A broad consensus on the non-racial political objectives of that struggle at the moment means that writers' organisations can devote more energy to innovative thinking in pursuit of alternative contributions to the search for radical solutions from the special perspective of the arts. There is a need to problematise aims, objectives, and projects of the organisations.

The latest writers' organisation is, of course, the Congress of South African Writers. To give a sense of some of the issues it will need to grapple with, it may be instructive to return to the dissolution of PEN (Johannesburg), an organisation that came very close, in form, to the Congress of South African Writers. Mafika Gwala's stand on the dissolution of PEN (Johannesburg) is now well known. Responding to the expressed discomfort of some black members of PEN over the fact of belonging to an organisation that had white members, Mafika Gwala's stand, as outlined here by Lionel Abrahams, was as follows:

> 'We are trapped in our class interests and don't know how to move forward, so we talk of colour . . . we are saying racist things'. Perhaps the community was erring, he continued: writers ought not to follow blindly but should give the lead; many issues bearing on the question of disbandment had not come to light, people were not talking out, somewhere the truth was being hidden.[15]

The account does not go on to outline the specific elaborations that Gwala may have made. But the essential thrust of his intervention was to introduce another dimension to the issue of membership, that is to say, within the context of the writers' movement: the question of class.

The other issue concerned the activities of PEN. Debates over the format of readings and workshops do not appear to have taken into account the diversity of interest and backgrounds within PEN itself. Such diversity could have been regarded as a pool of resources affording PEN a varied yet purposeful approach to confronting pressing cultural issues in South Africa. There was no reason for PEN not to have accommodated different kinds of format as long as each format was subjected to rigorous analysis. That way, the organisation would have been confronting practical issues of artistic strategy and its intended effects.

Perhaps Mike Kirkwood best describes the problem:

> We needed to look hard at ourselves and recognise that this potentially united yet broad-based movement of writers was

composed of writers using a great spectrum of artistic techniques and reaching very different audiences. We needed to grasp the fact that this diversity could be a tremendous source of strength and not necessarily a cause of division. Yet that effective solidarity could only be forged if we could spell out and agree upon the fundamental cultural values of the new society to which we as writers were committed. From that agreement could stem discussion of the different roles different writers could play in the realisation of those values – with the acceptance of the basic point that there would be different kinds of contribution.[16]

The Congress of South Africa Writers emerged out of the Writers' Forum in response to the growing mass-based democratic movement. It became very clear that writers had to do more than just meet and talk. Rather, they had to respond in more direct and practical ways, according to their particular artistic perspectives, to the demands of the moment. Coming at the moment when the momentum of struggle in South Africa has advanced considerably, COSAW has inherited from the broad democratic movement the capacity to confront squarely whatever contradictions may emerge in the course of its activities. The concept of democracy is a practical feature of discussion, broad consultation, and decision making. What COSAW has in place, consequently, is a method by which to solidify the organisation by legitimising critical dissent as well as the need to evaluate activities constantly. That has emerged as an important characteristic of comradeship.

The challenges are immense, but the most immediate one is to solidify the organisational sense in the manner indicated above, so that the way can be cleared for the Congress to address all matters that pertain to its interests. The present environment itself reinforces such a tendency. It is a climate within which exists an alternative press; efforts to establish an alternative philosophy of education embodied in the concept of 'people's' education; an increasing confidence in workers to produce art; a vigorous theatre movement;

an alternative medical association; and, above all, a strong workers' movement. Indeed, there has been no major aspect of South African society that has not been problematised. The writers' movement is situated there where it can draw a sustaining nourishment. It is also there that a rigorous confrontation of issues can take place constantly.

NOTES

1. Editorial, *Inkundla ya Bantu*, 31 July, 1948. See also Tim Couzens, *The New African: A Study of the Life and Work of H.I.E. Dhlomo*, (Johannesburg: Ravan Press, 1985), p.294.
2. A.P. Mda, 'African Academy of Arts', *Inkundla ya Bantu*, 24 July, 1947.
3. Tim Couzens, p.294.
4. Tim Couzens, p.295.
5. Lionel Abrahams, 'From Shakespeare House to the Laager: The Story of PEN (Johannesburg)', *Sesame*, p.5.
6. *Staffrider*, Vol.1, No.1, 1978.
7. Michael Vaughan, '*Staffrider* and Directions within Contemporary South African Literature' in *Literature and Society in South Africa*, Landeg White and Tim Couzens, (eds.), (New York: Longman, 1984), p.197.
8. *Staffrider*, Vol.2, No.3, 1978.
9. *Staffrider*, Vol.2, No.1, 1979.
10. Lionel Abrahams, p.7.
11. *Staffrider*, Vol.2, No.2, 1979.
12. Mike Kirkwood, 'Reflections on PEN', *Sesame*, Johannesburg, pp.22–6.
13. Achmat Dangor, *Sowetan*, 15 August, 1985.
14. Tim Couzens, p.259.
15. Lionel Abrahams, pp.18–19.
16. Mike Kirkwood, pp.24–5.

9

❖ ❖ ❖

APPENDIX:
THE NOMA AWARD ACCEPTANCE SPEECH

Sometime after the notorious Land Act of 1913 was passed in the white South African Parliament, a Lands Commission was established to look into the effects of the legislation. This Act, it will be remembered, was the one responsible for the granting of only 13 percent of land in South Africa to Africans, while the rest was to be the domain of the white man. One of the most critical observers of this phenomenon as it was unfolding was Sol Plaatje, one of the major figures in African writing in South Africa. His book, *Native Life in South Africa* (1916) is a landmark in the historiography on South African political repression. The book is remarkable not only for its impressive detailing of facts but also for its well considered rhetorical effects which express intelligent analysis, political clarity, and a strong moral purpose.

In his analysis of the Report of the Lands Commission, Sol Plaatje notes, among other observations:

> While the ruling whites, on the one hand, content themselves
> with giving contradictory definitions of their cruelty the native

This speech was made at the 1985 Zimbabwe Book Fair in Harare where the author was presented with the Noma Award for his collection *Fools and Other Stories*, published by Ravan Press, 1984.

sufferers, on the other, give no definitions of legislative phrases nor explanations of definitions. All they give expression to is their bitter suffering under the operation of what in their experience has proved to be the most ruthless law that ever disgraced the white man's rule in British South Africa. (pp.355–6)

Plaatje's observation here is of very special interest to me. He documents here one of the most debilitating effects of oppression: the depriving of the oppressed of any meaningful, significant intellectual life. Because they no longer have an effective hand in controlling history, they seem doomed to respond and seldom to initiate. Those doomed to respond seldom have the time to determine their real interests. That the capability to initiate action has been taken out of their hands implies also, that their ability to define has been drastically reduced. Plaatje notes here, how the African oppressed appear to have been reduced to the status of being mere bearers of witness. They do a good job of describing suffering; but they cannot define its quality. The ability to define is an intellectual capability more challenging, it seems to me, than the capability to describe. For to define is to understand, while to describe is merely to observe. Beyond mere observation, the path towards definition will begin only with an intellectual interest in what to observe and how to observe.

It seems to me that a large part of the African resistance to the evil of apartheid has, until recently, consisted of a largely descriptive documentation of suffering. And the bulk of the fiction, through an almost total concern with the political theme has, in following this tradition, largely documented rather than explained. Not that the political theme itself was not valid, on the contrary it is worth exploring almost as a duty. It was the manner of its treatment that became the subject of increasing dissatisfaction to me. Gradually, over a period of historical time, an image emerged and consolidated, as a result, of people completely destroyed, of passive people whose only reason for existing seemed to be to receive the sympathy of the world. To promote such an image in whatever manner, especially if such promotion also emanated from among the ranks of the oppressed themselves, was to promote a negation. It was to promote a fixed and unhistorical image with the result of obscuring the existence of a fiercely energetic and complex dialectic in the progress of human history. There was, in this attitude, a tragic denial of life.

I came to the realisation, mainly through the actual grappling with the form of fiction, that our literature ought to seek to move away from an easy pre-occupation with demonstrating the obvious existence of oppression. It exists. The task is to explore how and why people can survive under such harsh conditions. The mechanisms of survival and resistance that the people have devised are many and far from simple. The task is to understand them, and then to actively make them the material subject of our imaginative explorations. We have given away too much of our real and imaginative lives to the oppressor and his deeds. The task is to give our lives and our minds to the unlimited inventiveness of the suffering masses, and to give formal ideological legitimacy to their aspirations.

When I started writing, it was with the notion that art was an act of self-expression. But I realised that it was something else: it was an act of knowledge through self-confrontation. But it is a self-confrontation that takes place within the community of people who emerge out of one's pen, as it were. I realised that self-expression was not the essence but merely the end product of art. What I found in the struggle with the form of fiction was that next to their material interests, and surrounding those interests, people maintain a strong and vital ethical interest in the conduct of human affairs. This interest is expressed in their public, or in their private lives, and it involves a range of vital human concerns. It involves questions of loyalty and betrayal; of bravery and cowardice; of anxiety and contentment; of rigidity and adaptation; of cruelty and compassion; of honour and dishonour; of pride and humility, and a variety of similarly conflicting attitudes all of which excite a very strong human, ethical interest. I felt, as a result, that I had to attempt to bring into the active consciousness of the oppressed, through a total evocation of their life, an active philosophical interest in the complex dialectic of human existence. The very resources of living should constitute the material essence of the search for personal and social meaning.

All of this means that the task of the new generation of South African writers is to help to extend the material range of intellectual and imaginative interest as far as the subject of life under oppression is concerned. It is to look for that area of cultural autonomy and the laws of its dynamism that no oppressor can ever get at; to define that area, and, with purposeful insidiousness, to assert its irrepressible hegemony during the actual process of struggle. That hegemony will necessarily be an organic one: involving the entire range of human activity. Only on this condition can a new creative, and universally meaningful democratic civilisation be built in South Africa.

This year's award, I believe, is in essence not for the two books selected. It is rather, in recognition of perhaps the beginning of a new era on our continent, both the large area that is independent, and that small remaining part that is still locked in struggle with oppression. Whereas we have documented the quality of our lives; whereas we have largely diagnosed the prevalent social illness, we now have to embark upon a fundamental re-evaluation of methods not just in fiction, but in all areas of human activity. I have learned, in the craft of fiction for example, that the difference between writers is not so much in the subjects of their writings: the range of subject matter is relatively limited. Rather, it is in the inventiveness of treatment, in the sharpening of insight, and in the deepening of consciousness. The material life of Africa should be given a new formal articulation that will enlarge intellectual interest and expand the possibilities of the imagination. It is a re-evaluation which, I believe, should result in a profound philosophical transformation of the African consciousness, a consciousness that should and must endure.

10

❖ ❖ ❖

APPENDIX:
INTERVIEW WITH NJABULO S. NDEBELE

Albie Sachs's approach in 'Preparing Ourselves for Freedom' is similar to your approach in 'Turkish Tales and Some Thoughts on South African Fiction' (Staffrider, 6, 1, 1984), 'The Rediscovery of the Ordinary' (Journal of Southern African Studies, 12, 2, April 1986) and 'Redefining Relevance' (Pretexts, 1, 1, Winter 1989). What is your response to Sachs's paper?

The major controversy around Sachs's paper has tended to focus on why his statement has attracted so much attention, and why other people's similar statements have not. It's not a very important question in my view. The reception of Albie Sachs's paper indicates that it's important *where* you say something. Most of my pronouncements came out in academic journals – with a fairly restricted circulation. So discussions of those pronouncements tended to take place largely in the restricted world of academia, as well as amongst writers and other cultural activists. But the discussion does not appear to have filtered down to the rest of the public to any significant extent. Obviously there's a difference between the academic world

This interview was originally published in *Exchanges: South African Writing in Transition*, edited by Duncan Brown and Bruno van Dyk (Pietermaritzburg: University of Natal Press, 1991).

and the one in which Albie Sachs was operating, the context of the ANC seminar. The ANC's views on culture, as well as on other aspects of South African life, are a matter of intense public interest. Academics may very well envy that level of interest, but its existence, under the circumstances, cannot be disputed.

It should not be surprising then that a pronouncement of the nature which Albie Sachs made should become a notable historical event. It has nothing to do with the depth or otherwise of the pronouncement, but with the fact that it was made, that it went against the then established view, and that many of us had been talking about the same subject. I think we should be relieved that Albie Sachs intervened and has managed to popularise the debate from within the ANC, and that it has subsequently entered the public domain. His pronouncement, it now seems, is what many people secretly desired to say, but were afraid to say it. *That* is the historical significance of the pronouncement as an event, rather than who made it first. The latter is a matter of dates, while the former is a significant political event which makes it possible for all that has been said before, but suppressed, to re-emerge for further discussion.

Christopher van Wyk and Nadine Gordimer, particularly, had been saying something similar.

One of the reasons why the voices of Nadine Gordimer and Chris van Wyk may not have made such an impact is that they made the interventions at a time when it was very risky. At that time you could very easily be misinterpreted and targeted as a 'sell-out'. The necessity of closing ranks meant the suppression of criticism, even if that criticism could strengthen the movement in the long run. In other words, the controls that the state imposed on everyone, we also imposed on ourselves. Historically it is perhaps understandable that when you are powerless, as an act of survival you want to make sure that you keep your group intact, because any possible disintegration reinforces powerlessness. Your options are limited, and you have to make some tragic choices. In the fight for freedom, you may experience the need to contain freedom within your own organisation. You maintain group cohesion, but at a price. It should be recognised when such a historically determined situation becomes a threat to the very survival of the group. This is not a moral issue, it is a matter of survival.

In two of your essays ('The Rediscovery of the Ordinary' and 'Redefining Relevance') the titles indicate that you have for a long time been inviting a reassessment of the cultural production in this country. What are the origins of your particular cultural stance?

I think it comes out of my own creative writing. I was exposed at a very early age to literature written by black South Africans, albeit those who were banned – my father had quite a collection hidden in boxes. Of course I read many of the magazines, *Drum*, *Classic* and others, which were available at home. When I discovered an interest in writing, I had already developed some attitudes about what I liked. I had read so much of what one could call 'protest literature' that I reproduced it in my own early unpublished poetry, as well as in some plays which I wrote at high school in Swaziland.

There were other writers who influenced me tremendously. There was a time in my writing when I was fascinated with children, and I read books such as *Lord of the Flies*, *Portrait of the Artist as a Young Dog*, and practically everything by Dylan Thomas, James Joyce, and Bernardo Honwana, the Mozambican who wrote wonderful short stories. These are works of a very high quality from the point of view of technique and theme. I became interested in exploring art beyond merely reflecting reality as it was, because we are all familiar with it, we can see the evidence of oppression. I became more interested in how oppression affects people in their day to day lives, what it does to the fabric of family life, how it affects individual ambitions and aspirations, how it contributes to the way we rationalise about things, how we tend to avoid personal responsibility, because it's easy to say apartheid caused it. These are some of the truths I felt we had to grapple with.

One of my latest stories – 'Death of a Son' – deals with township unrest, the phenomenon of police invading the townships and lobbing teargas canisters at random into houses. A little child dies in the process. The child's mother is a journalist, and the father is a young man who is doing very well in an American company. They live very comfortably. But this random attack affects them. It's easy to write a story that concentrates on the anger of it all. But I felt that we've seen a lot of that, and concentrated rather on how the incident affected their personal relationship, as man and wife. They triumph in the end, but the incident brings out the nature of their relationship: it is discovered to be somewhat superficial. At the end of the story they come to terms with themselves – there's a greater self-knowledge – and the marriage, from that point on, is based on a more mature understanding of their limitations as well as their strengths.

It's a long way of answering your question, but my experience of my own creative writing found its way into my criticism.

Beyond that, I have never forgotten Herbert Read's dictum which I came across and memorised in my last year at high school. It goes something like, 'the distortion of truth-to-nature is at the same time an intensification of natural vitality'. I liked that. It summed up for me the relationship between art and society. Herbert Read was discussing distortion in modern art. I was fascinated by that because it freed me from the tendency to 'copy' reality.

On at least two occasions you have argued that, far from being a literature of defiance, the literature of protest has been a literature of powerlessness: in 'Turkish Tales' you stated that 'the psychology of the slogan in these [oppressive] circumstances is the psychology of intellectual powerlessness', and in 'The Rediscovery of the Ordinary' you stated that protest literature 'is the literature of the powerless identifying the key factor responsible for their powerlessness'. Would you elaborate on the reasons informing this critique?

I've already covered this to some extent in my response to the previous question, but there's a shift in emphasis here in the reference to 'powerlessness'. I called this 'the literature of powerlessness' because there were many things that made black people feel powerless: they had no control over the system of education; they had very little say in the way the economy was run, or in government matters; they had absolutely no say in where they could stay or build a house. They experienced life as endless prohibition. This does tend to affect the manner in which you conceptualise intellectually, the problems which you confront, and the extent to which you can analyse those problems. Sometimes in expressing your anger or bitterness, the very expression becomes an index of how powerless you actually are so that you reproduce your powerlessness even in articulating it. It's something that is difficult to get out of when you are caught in it.

In the opening paragraph of 'Redefining Relevance' there's the metaphor of the train that's running and passing every station. The difference is that the driver of the train is not the *train*, so he is immediately aware that he's in trouble. But when you are caught in an entrenched manner of thinking, it is difficult to objectify yourself. The way out of the powerlessness is obviously to be involved in struggle, and this is what people have been doing in the last forty years with an increasing degree of confidence. We are now at the stage where to talk about your powerlessness is no longer an indication of how powerless you actually are. At the same time that you articulate your powerlessness, you address the question of how to end this state of affairs in order to become a free person. There is a great deal of confidence, now, in the ability of people to influence the course of events. That makes for entirely new possibilities of intellectual and artistic development, of just feeling free – that you can move wherever you like – that the page of history is wide open for all sorts of stories to be written.

What is the enduring contribution of the literature of protest, especially as we move into what would appear to be a new 'literary period'?

From a literary point of view, the most observable, lasting attribute of the literature of protest is the sheer sense of drama in the stories.

Everything is expressed in very stark, dramatic terms. That sense of story-telling has persisted, and is something to cherish, irrespective of the complaints about repetition, the reappearance of the same characters and so on. These stories also remain as documents that testify to the moral vision of the oppressor.

Perhaps one of the paradoxes of South African literature, and even of South African culture in general, is that, despite (or perhaps owing to) oppression, the literature (to single out but one form of cultural expression) that has been produced by South African writers is both vital and varied.

If we consider other art forms as well as literature, I agree that our cultural production has been very varied. If you look back, you'll find that South Africans have been at the forefront of developments in Africa in many fields. Very early – in 1912 – one of the greatest political movements in Africa began. South Africans started writing a long time ago: in the nineteenth century newspapers were already being written in the Cape; in Lesotho, which was also a centre of much publishing in African languages, the great novels of Mofolo and Sekese appeared. Dave Coplan, in his book *In Township Tonight!*, shows how similar developments were taking place in the areas of music and dance. By the 1930s, we had really produced a lot of writing compared with the rest of the continent. In the realm of the short story, big names like Mphahlele, Lewis Nkosi, Nat Nakasa, Alex La Guma and Dennis Brutus generally dominated African literature.

Round about the late fifties and early sixties many black South Africans went into exile, often to teach in West or East Africa – so we took skills to the rest of the continent, and made our contribution. But things have changed now – Nigeria is probably the biggest producer of literature – because the vast majority of the population of South Africa was held in check, and so the creativity that could have burst forth was stifled. But in spite of oppression, people have been able to express themselves in various forms and keep the traditions alive. In music, certainly, we have reached a high level of achievement, and the indications are that it is still moving forward. There's still much to be done in literature and art. But the environment now is permissive of further developments.

In what way do you think the changing political climate in the country has affected the position of writers?

It's difficult to talk about roles in a changing environment. One can only talk about how the writer can use the freer environment to develop himself or herself; maybe somewhere along the line a role will emerge. I think the way in which the new environment can be used is that writers have to develop an attitude towards their art which makes them artists (I use the word deliberately as opposed to something like 'cultural workers'), because in all fields of human endeavour there's a lack of skills amongst blacks. We're in a period in which, now that we have made these gains, the only way in which we can consolidate and move forward is to acquire skills. And writers are part of this process. For the writer it means having a passionate interest in education, knowing more about the world in which you live, extending your knowledge about people tirelessly, and reading other writers as much as you can. Then you have to develop the discipline to write, which means giving up a lot of other things, in the same way that for any discipline you have to put aside time, develop habits of work that will enable you to complete your tasks.

Now, let us assume that you've done these things. You then become aware that there's a whole world out there for you. Nobody will tell you how to write your story. You can experiment with literary technique as much as you like, you can play around with point of view, you can put the end of the story at the beginning and retrace the events. You can also write about things that people were afraid to write about.

I have just finished reading a marvellous novel which is to me the ultimate vindication – Achmat Dangor's *Z Town Trilogy*. He has written about a so-called Coloured/Indian community in a manner which has never been done before, exposing its contradictions, rationalisations, sincerities and insincerities. But even when he is most critical, he writes about his people with a great deal of love and compassion. So the worst character also deserves some respect, paradoxically. There are also characters of different political persuasions arguing vociferously and revealing in the process their insincerities and posturing.

This kind of thing hasn't been consistently done before. I hope it will make for a more open, sensitive society, more caring, compassionate people, because we are no longer afraid of addressing also the ugliness, and we realise that the human being is a very complex thing – even the most heroic people have insecurities that enhance their heroism when they are revealed. So we don't lose anything by opening up. On the contrary, I think we become better people. Perhaps this is the role of the writer, indeed, to reveal the currents of human interaction in his or her community, as openly, as frankly, and yet as lovingly as possible in writing about them.

There is a sense that Sachs's paper is problematic as a policy document on culture in that at no stage does it attempt a thorough critique of revolutionary culture or any other culture for that matter. With this in mind would you speculate on the value of Sachs's paper as a foundation for cultural production?

I don't think we should attempt to make it anything more than what it was, which was an intervention at a particular point in time into the cultural debate. We had someone expressing his views about what he feels ought to be done. I don't think Albie Sachs set out to present a challenge to academics, to offer an arcane theory of literature. It's not fair to look for that kind of thing in his essay. This goes back to the very first question that you asked, when I said that we will only go back to Albie Sachs's paper when we discuss the history of the development of criticism. It's an important document because it was a very significant intervention. Whether Sachs goes on to talk about the dynamics of culture or not is not the issue.

You are a literary critic as well as a writer. On what do you base your criticism?

The only body of intellectual knowledge that I can say I owe a lot to is the dialectical approach to human society, because I still find that (in spite of all that's been said of the decline of the Eastern bloc) as an intellectual body of knowledge that tradition offers theories of society that have a very high explanatory value. Starting from that point, I have read a lot in critical theory. As students of literature we all start from Plato and find our way to Deconstruction. But in my own criticism I try to look at the South African literary situation from an interventionist point of view. Whatever I take from other theories is eclectic. I'm not conscious of pursuing a particular point of view. I prefer to look at the situation as it is, subject it as rigorously as possible to my own intellectual scrutiny, and arrive at insights on the basis of what I find and the critical experience that I have.

So I was quite surprised by Tony Morphet's recent article in *Pretexts* (2, 1, Winter 1990). He puts my criticism in a certain tradition. When I wrote 'Redefining Relevance' I was far from thinking about structuralism or post-structuralism. I prefer an open-ended approach, tackling everything as I see it at a particular point in time. If what results carries a lot of other traditions, then I will not deny that I may have been influenced by them.

What is your response to worker poets like Mzwakhe Mbuli or Alfred Qabula?

The hidden assumption behind this question is that claims are being made or have been made about the quality of work of these poets which cannot be held up against the actual work.

You will also recall some of the early debates once African literature began to be taken seriously. There was a very strong view, very arrogantly projected, that there's no such phenomenon as African literature: 'They don't write like T.S. Eliot or Wallace Stevens. Literature is *English* literature.' I emphasise English literature because the people who were propagating this view were not exposed to other traditions of literature – Russian, Arabian, Chinese, etc. Just because it was the tradition they knew, they tended to universalise it. So the questioning of the value of the worker poets' work is not unrelated to this attitude.

Once we have dealt with that, we are still left with the poetry which has to be evaluated on its own merits. My point of view would be that there is not a single worker poet, considering the milieu that they work in and the kind of audience they have in mind, who's not trying to ensure that the next poem that he or she does is better than the last one. Consequently, in order for us to evaluate their work, we'll have to find out what the worker poets' own concept of literary development is. You'll probably find, at the end of the day, that their idea of what constitutes a successful work of art is not very different from our own.

I would say that the worker poets have had a role to play: they brought literature to the factories when this could not have been done before. Who else could have done that? If we don't like that phenomenon, then implicitly we don't like the fact that as many people as possible have to be involved in culture. We must diversify the conditions in which people can appreciate art, and this is what worker poets did. The challenge is to push that forward, and to do it in a manner that will involve the widest community. In the townships, for instance, very little was done to enhance cultural activity. You certainly don't see the theatres, cinemas, libraries or schools that we find in the white community. So I look at the contribution of the worker poets from that point of view.

This is not to say that they have not written some poems which, when you read them the following day, you find totally flat. But it should be noted that most of the worker poets are oral poets, so you can't really evaluate their poems on the written page in the absence of the audience, the poet's gestures, and modulation of his/ her voice.

Lastly, I think that the worker poets simply add to the range of artistic choices that should be available to the community.

What do you think will be the role of literature in the country in the future?

The role of literature will be to make us conscious of the multiplicity and complexity of human experience. It is unlike other art forms. In music, when you like a song, you experience a sense of well-being which you cannot easily articulate. But in literature the attempt is made to bring out everything explicitly. We are therefore made more conscious through language of the way we can interact with one another. I think that is the function of literature. So it becomes important that there should be all kinds of writing, from Mzwakhe to Coetzee.

This brings us to the question of language. I recently attended a performance of Mothobi Mutloatse's latest play. What was interesting was the way language was used in the play. There was English – of course most of the play was in English – then Zulu, then *tsotsi-taal*, then Sotho, and so on. I'm not sure how many white people in the audience were able to appreciate some of the jokes because they were not familiar with the language. Whereas (and this takes us back to your question about the varied nature of our cultural production in spite of oppression) at school we were forced to learn Afrikaans, Zulu, Sotho, the lot, and we now find that this is an advantage for us. It just shows the extent to which whites have to learn more about other cultures before they can appreciate the richness of the play.

So language becomes a key factor in opening up avenues of expression that previously were closed off. We need to come up with a language policy that will enable South Africans to speak as many languages as possible, while maintaining a sense of efficiency in the public service. Then the literature in other languages will be opened up, and will develop. We should avoid the tendency to think of literature as literature written in English or Afrikaans. There is a vast body of literature written in other languages which ought to be placed centre stage as well, so that South Africans can have a greater appreciation of the wealth of culture in their country.